HOW TO BE A FREELAN

In this Series

Other titles in preparation

BE A FREELANCE
SALES AGENT

Your path to a more rewarding future

Terry James

How To Books

Cartoons by Mike Flanagan

British Library Cataloguing-in-Publication data
A catalogue record for this book is available from the British Library.

© Copyright 1995 by Terry James.

First published in 1995 by How To Books Ltd, Plymbridge House,
Estover Road, Plymouth PL6 7PZ, United Kingdom.
Tel: (01752) 735251/695745. Fax: (01752) 695699.
Telex: 45635.

Note: The material contained in this book is set out in good faith for
general guidance and no liability can be accepted for loss or expense
incurred as a result of relying in particular circumstances on statements
made in the book. The laws and regulations are complex and liable to
change, and readers should check the current position with the relevant
authorities before making personal arrangements.

Typeset by Kestrel Data, Exeter.
Printed and bound in Great Britain by The Cromwell Press,
Broughton Gifford, Melksham, Wiltshire.

Contents

List of Illustrations

IS THIS YOU?

Are you a salesperson in one of these industries?

Double glazing	Packing machinery	Toiletries
Insurance	Paints & coatings	Jewellery
Garden supplies	Machine tools	Ethical drugs
Household furniture	Electrical goods	Office furniture
Plumbing goods	Financial services	Computers
Leather goods	Fashion	Tableware
Office flooring	Stationery	Shelving
Catering supplies	Beauty supplies	Golf equipment
Cleaning systems	Floorcoverings	Hobbies
Exhibition systems	Picture frames	Knitware
Building materials	Nameplates	Security
Rubber stamps	Labels	Lifts
Kitchen equipment	Oils and grease	Plastic mouldings
Hand tools	Bookselling	Pensions
Transport	Housewares	Hospital equipment

Foreword

As the Managing Director of a small but rapidly expanding business, I am asked to do lots of things during any given week. One of the nicest things I have been asked to do this week is to write the foreword to Terry's book.

There is a distinct shortage of sales agents and, if we define that further, good sales agents, then they are as rare as hen's teeth! If you think you would like to become an agent and you have the skill and confidence, then do it. I know this book will help you.

Back in the '70s, I was sales director for a division of the GKN Group. My department numbered 110, of which 75 were reps out on the road. Times have changed, the days of the big company with the mega salesforce have largely gone. Post-Thatcher Britain is made up of thousands of small businesses, all of whom have one thing in common. In order to survive and grow they need to sell their goods or services. The question is how?

That was the situation I was in when I decided to form this business, almost six years ago. I decided to sell my products through a nationwide network of sales agents. This proved to be one of my better decisions. It provided two major advantages. Firstly it linked my selling costs directly to my sales revenue, and, secondly, as sales agents are business people in their own right, they tend to think commercially, are self motivated and self managing.

If you want to know 'How To' the best way is to listen to an experienced enthusiast on the subject. That is why I can think of no better person that Terry James to undertake this book.

David Williams
Managing Director,
Bilco (UK) Ltd,
Bury St Edmunds

Preface

I became a freelance sales agent by accident. Having risen to management status in sales and having been through a spate of redundancies, it was a case of 'the higher you rise the further you fall'. I was fed up with my future being in the hands of others.

In searching for a solution to this problem, my thoughts naturally turned towards self employment. Having just reared a family my capital was very limited so starting my own company making or leasing out widgets was out of the question. An evaluation of my skills showed that my main skill lay in my lifetime experience in sales. But how was I to capitalise on these skills without working for someone else?

A chance occurrence happened at that point. A previous colleague revealed that his company was seeking a sales agent in my area. As I was unemployed at the time I had nothing to lose by attending the interview. I was most impressed by the company and its products and was offered the agency.

Realising that it would take some time to get established, cover my expenses and make a profit, I set myself an extremely tight budget. I arranged a small overdraft with my bank and accepted the agency. As luck would have it I walked into a major order for the product almost immediately and I was hooked on being a sales agent.

That was some ten years ago. I wish I could say it has been easy all the way but it has not. There have been good and bad times but that is true of life in general. I am not earning a fortune but I have something I prize above everything, my independence. I am out of the rat race. I am not judged by whether my face fits into an organisation or how I get on with the boss. I am judged by how much I sell. If I don't sell I don't eat! It is as simple as that.

I could earn considerably more if I worked harder but, approaching retiring age, I am starting to wind down. That is why

I wanted to write this book, to pass on some of my experience to anybody who is thinking of becoming a freelance sales agent but is afraid of the unknown.

Terry James

Publisher's note
There are many women sales agents and the use of the word 'he' throughout this book is not meant to imply an exclusively male presence.

1
Becoming a Sales Agent

In this chapter we will examine:

- the sales agent's role
- potential earnings
- self discipline needs
- the lack of age and fitness barriers
- experience in sales
- avoiding risks.

WHAT IS A SALES AGENT?

A sales agent is a freelance, self employed sales person who works, usually alone, for perhaps several, non competing, companies and obtains orders for those companies and is paid a commission on those orders. Each arrangement with each company is usually referred to as an agency. A sales agent sometimes describes the company he is working for as his principal. Sometimes a retainer is paid to the sales agent but this usually comes with strings attached.

He usually works in a specific area of industry or commerce and usually within geographical limits. There are no limits to the types of industry and commerce where sales agents are found. Many companies use teams of sales agents to get national coverage and some companies use a mixture of employed salespeople and sales agents.

The sales agent is playing an ever increasing role in UK business. Many companies are looking hard at their costs and realising the real benefits of placing their sales efforts in the hands of the ever increasing number of competent and professional sales agents that are available today. In the United States, Europe and many other parts of the world, owing to the large areas involved, the use of sales agents is quite normal. Normally only the major companies in these countries employ their own salesmen.

Sales agent or distributor, the difference?
There is a possible misunderstanding in the difference between a sales agent and a distributor.

A distributor:

- purchases and holds stock
- solicits orders
- delivers the orders
- invoices the goods or service
- takes the credit risk
- makes a profit on the transaction

A sales agent:

- solicits orders
- passes orders to the principal
- earns an agreed commission on those orders.

Most sales agents consider themselves to be at the pinnacle of their sales career. They rely on their professionalism, salesmanship and customer relationships to earn their living. In return it is theoretically possible to enjoy an income far in excess of that usually earned by a company salesperson. The only limit to the size of their earnings is the amount of time, effort and salesmanship they put in. Not for them the petty squabbles, rivalry and jealousy that arise when such earnings are within a company structure.

Apart from the potential earnings the satisfaction derived from being the boss and running the company their way must be taken into account.

An inexpensive way of being your own boss
Becoming a freelance sales agent is probably one of the least expensive and easiest routes for someone with some sales experience to have their own business. If you have a telephone, some form of transport, including public transport, and are reasonably competent at selling you can become a successful sales agent with

all the pride, independence and earnings that are part of that success.

Remember, once you become a sales agent you will never ever become redundant. Principals may go bankrupt, but you, wisely working for a range of principals, can carry on and replace the failed principal with your own choice in your own time.

WILL I MAKE A SALES AGENT?

The first and most important requirement for success as a sales agent is some sales experience. It is very difficult trying to cope with the inevitable mistakes made whilst learning to sell and, at the same time, trying to earn a living purely on how much you can sell.

Lots of companies use inexperienced people as employed salespeople on the basis that they have demonstrated some potential, they can train them into their own sales methods and they come relatively cheaply. The benefit to the inexperienced salesperson is that they make their mistakes and learn their craft at someone else's expense.

Figure 1 is a list of desirable attributes of a sales agent but do not take these too literally. Many very successful agents are short on several of these qualities.

Self discipline: it's your time and money

Self discipline is an essential quality. It is easy to find an excuse for not going out to call on prospective customers and to spend time instead at home on various administrative jobs. That eventually spells disaster.

Be prepared to:

- maximise your time with customers
- spend some spare time on administration
- be self motivating
- not turn colds into flu
- set your own targets.

Persistence and tenacity are other requirements. The going will get hard at times, especially while you are building the agency up. The ability to fight back after a major setback is a necessary

Do you have some or all of these attributes?

	YES	NO
Some sales experience	☐	☐
Independently minded	☐	☐
Some initial capital	☐	☐
Versatile	☐	☐
Mobile	☐	☐
Self-disciplined	☐	☐
Determined	☐	☐
Established connections	☐	☐
Decisive	☐	☐
Reasonably healthy	☐	☐

Fig. 1. Desirable attributes of a sales agent.

requirement for a sales agent. Setbacks come in varying forms, for example the failure of a principal, the loss of a large order or customer. When this happens you do not have the luxury of blaming others and still taking home a salary. You have to get out there and replace that lost income, with a smile on your face.

Most setbacks come in the early stages of your career as a sales agent. Experience teaches you how to avoid the most common causes of disappointment but they will always be there.

Doing it your way

To some people it comes as a culture shock not to have colleagues around them to discuss matters regarding daily business life. To a certain extent you will have to become a loner but, as will be shown later, it is not a completely lonely life.

Making decisions alone will become second nature to you. You will make good and bad decisions. Luckily those decisions are yours and you can blame only yourself if it is a bad decision.

Make a decision before the money runs out

The absence of initial financial pressure is very helpful in the first stages of becoming a sales agent. The need to earn, and earn extremely quickly, can cause problems in the initial period. If you are relying on redundancy money or other finance to tide you over the lean first months of setting up an agency, make the decision before the finance is exhausted.

Everybody has come across salespeople who have to get the order there and then. They look desperate and it shows. The sales agent must have time to build customer confidence in him and the several product ranges he sells. This route usually leads to greater sales than can be achieved by a company salesperson who is just offering one product range.

ARE THERE AGE LIMITS?

The selling profession has no age barriers so becoming a sales agent follows this rule. It has the further advantage that sales agents sometimes carry on till a ripe old age. In salaried selling jobs an employer sometimes chooses younger salespeople because he can mould them to his liking and they probably come cheaper or work faster. With a sales agent the principal is not paying you for how many calls you put in or how hard you work, he is paying you for the orders you bring in. It matters not to him whether you are 20 or 90 years old, he still pays the same commission.

It is a fact that many agents carry on working for many years after the normal retirement age even if they do not need the money. They might cut down the number of agencies held or the distances travelled but they find it is a way of life they cannot completely give up. Sometimes it is the lack of a decent pension that prompts them to carry on working.

HOW FIT DO I HAVE TO BE?

Obviously the fitter you are the better you will be able to carry out your major function, contacting customers and obtaining orders. Nevertheless many agents are successful despite medical problems that would probably deter their employment as a paid salesman.

Do tell any prospective principal of your condition and how you aim to get round it from the outset. If you can demonstrate a positive attitude towards your disorder and show him that your sales will not be affected overall, it should not go against you. They will respect your frankness.

WHAT ARE THE REWARDS?

Before you can make this decision you must get some information on the average amount of commission normally paid in your chosen area of operation. Commissions vary enormously but do tend towards the general rule that if there is much easy and quick repeat business to be had then the commission rate is lower than, at the other end of the scale, where the sale is a one off and may take many months, even years to bear fruit.

The commission rates also vary widely within any particular industry. However, in general they will average out at around 10 per cent. If you have been working as a salesman in the industry where you intend to become a sales agent, as a quick calculation, take an estimated possible yearly turnover and 10 per cent of that, your commission, will be your theoretical income less, of course, your expenses which are dealt with later.

The income tax benefit

A major advantage of being self-employed is in the system of taxation. Generally speaking the allowance for expenses is far more generous than with an employed person.

The tax benefits include:

- being taxed only on the actual profits made
- wholly business expenses are tax deductible
- pension payments are tax deductible
- losses can be carried forward to a new tax year
- assets such as cars have a depreciation allowance.

Nevertheless estimating your income in the early days is extremely difficult and not an exact art. It is easier to estimate your running expenses on a monthly basis, then add your estimate of how much you need to live on as a minimum. This figure represents your needed income derived from sales at, say, 10 per cent commission.

Do not forget that your first month's income from sales will probably be nil and should increase from that point. You must set yourself some targets for sales, especially in the early months, as they are pointers towards your ultimate goal of paying your expenses, taking a wage and making a profit on top. Do not expect to make a profit in the first few months.

WHAT ARE THE RISKS?

The major way of minimising risk is, as with insurance companies, spreading the risks. Most sales agents represent several, non competing companies, sometimes in the same business area and sometimes spread the risk even further by taking agencies on in different areas of business. In this way, even if an agency should not work out as you hoped for whatever reason, there are other agencies to fall back on.

The single agency lure

A major potential pitfall is to concentrate on one agency only. It may be that their service or product is easy to sell and you can make an easy income from them to the detriment of any other agencies you hold.

Consider the following:

- company policies towards agents do change
- try to have short, medium and long term income
- get your principals to accept your other agencies
- be prepared to weed out non earning agencies.

It is not uncommon for sales agents to build a company's sales up to a point where it is cheaper for them to pay an employed salesperson rather than pay extremely large commission cheques.

Another strategy is to spread your agencies over short, medium and long term sales. Too much of either type can lead to risks. For example, short term business is usually quick selling, quick return and highly competitive. If your short term business principal becomes uncompetitive you have already laid down medium and long term strategies which give you time to await his return to competitiveness without losing your livelihood. At the other extreme too much reliance on long term business can lead to large gaps in your income and disappointment when that order you have been working on for many months is cancelled.

Most realistic principals will acknowledge your desire to work for other principals as well. Many of them could not realistically expect you to earn a living from their goods or services alone. It means that you will stay with them even if the going gets temporarily hard.

QUESTIONS AND ANSWERS

Q. *You use the words 'sales agents' but I have never ever heard the term in the industry I work in?*

A. There are many descriptions such as 'commission only salesperson', 'agent', 'sales consultant' etc, but for simplicity we will describe all the activities outlined in this book as sales agents.

Q. *It all sounds very easy and the selling side is no different to what I have been doing for employers for some time, but what are the pitfalls?*

A. The pitfalls will be discussed as we get further into the book. The major pitfall at this point is that it must be realised from the outset that a high degree of self-discipline will be called for. You will not have anyone chasing you. **You** are the boss.

Q. *What is the worst setback I could have initially?*
A. Probably the worst thing that can happen to you is that one of your principals' business fails, owing you a lot of commission. How to minimise this risk is dealt with later, but not relying on one principal alone is the major way to limit the damage.

CASE STUDIES

Charles comes up against age discrimination

Charles Gann is a 52 year old sales manager who has just been made redundant for the third time in ten years. He is a good manager of himself and other people and his redundancy has not been due to any shortcomings on his part. He is married and his children have grown up and are not a liability. He has a large house but the mortgage is nearly paid. He has some savings that he is prepared to risk.

He has an excellent track record as a sales manager and a salesman and can present himself well. He has made many job applications but has only been offered a couple of interviews that were not successful. He puts the lack of success down to his age, having been sometimes interviewed by much younger people for these jobs. He is becoming rather despondent.

Dennis is frustrated by lack of promotion

Dennis Wilson felt he was losing ground in the promotion race. He is a 30 year old salesman who is dissatisfied with the lack of promotion that he feels is due to him, having had an excellent sales record with both the companies he has worked for since leaving school. He is married, has two young children, a large mortgage and a large overdraft.

He feels that his earnings are being limited by his lack of promotion. His present company, like a lot of companies, feels it has to limit the range of salaries earned by its salespeople to avoid disharmony and jealousy. It has long been his ambition to be his own boss but he cannot think what to make and sell. He feels that his sales abilities are far greater than those of the people who manage him. This has led to a confrontational attitude in his dealings with his company.

Samantha is looking for a way back into work

Samantha Grey is looking for full time employment but feels she is getting nowhere. She had enjoyed and was extremely successful in a selling job many years ago. She is a 45 year old recently divorced lady who has spent the last 18 years raising a family and building a home. She now wants to re-enter the business world but has no skills other than her, rather dated, selling skills to offer. After several unsuccessful interviews for a position as a sales representative she thinks her sex and maturity have counted against her. Samantha is a lively, active lady who gets on well with people.

She has her own car and is not short of money. Her need is for a job that will allow her to work the hours she wants, to allow her to follow her hobbies.

Discussion points

1. Each of the people in the case studies have certain attributes that could lead them into an excellent career as a sales agent. Can you spot them?

2. What attributes do you think you have that will make you a good sales agent?

3. How would you describe the difference between a sales agent and a distributor?

2
Why the Principal Needs You

This chapter is about:

- your 'initial cost' benefit
- the fixed cost of sales advantage
- the immediate new customer base
- assisting product orientated principals
- recognising your disadvantages.

SAVING THE PRINCIPAL MONEY

The cost to companies of actually employing and putting sales-people on the road is very considerable and variable. These costs are incurred before the salesperson has even set foot in the door of a customer let alone shown a profit on the orders he gets. If the salesperson is ineffective it may take many months to find this out, but salary and costs have to be paid during this time.

The costs of employing salespeople include:

- monthly salary
- vehicle costs
- fuel costs
- telephone expenses
- national insurance
- hotel costs
- non productive initial period
- possible sales management costs.

Because these costs and the income from sales are variable the company cannot calculate the true cost of a salesperson in its prices. They usually make an educated guess. Always remember, your sales are fixed cost sales. All they have to do is add your fixed commission to their costs.

You are offering:

- no initial costs
- a fixed percentage of commission
- no sales no pay
- no sales management costs.

As you are usually working with other principals, you are spreading your costs over perhaps several agencies.

Making the principal aware of these benefits

A considerable number of principals who are offering agencies do not even realise this major benefit or others that we shall mention. They tend to think in the general terms that they cannot afford to employ salespeople and that sales agents are cheaper. If you are fighting hard to gain a wanted agency remember to sell these and other benefits hard to the principal.

Remember, you already have something to sell, **your services**. It is essential that you know the benefits of your services in order to sell them to a prospective principal.

BRINGING THE PRINCIPAL A NEW CUSTOMER BASE

Most sales agents choose to work in the industry they have sold in for some time. The sales agent therefore has customers who have been visited for a long time and who buy regularly. Even if the agent does not necessarily do business with a company, he knows it exists, who is the decision maker and that it is a prospect. This is a major benefit to a principal. You are bringing him an extra, new, potential, customer base immediately. Also, as you have probably built up a customer base with your other agencies, you are giving him access to them.

You could bring him:

- market knowledge in your chosen area
- access to your existing customer base
- your credibility attached to his offer.

Your credibility as a selling point

It is a fact that 'people buy people', meaning that most buyers, all things being equal, buy from salespeople they like and respect. You as a sales agent will come to know this more than most salespeople. Respect should always be your aim. Most sales agents build up a base of existing customers who buy, or are at least prepared to listen about, further products from that sales agent. They respect the agent's judgement.

If you are a new sales agent or are selling into an unknown market area, you do not have this advantage, but at least your principal will not be paying out a salary while you find out who the buyers are.

ASSISTING PRODUCT BIASED COMPANIES

Many companies are what could be described as product biased. This means they are very good at producing the product or service but are not very skilful at selling. The owners probably do not come from a selling background or they formed the company in the hope that sales would just appear. Other companies may have spent too much money developing the product or service and do not have enough left over to employ salespeople. As an agent, you have a tremendous amount to offer such companies.

Your advantages

- You can bring in immediate selling skills.
- You can advise on how to present the offer.
- There may be flexibility in commission rates.

The disadvantages to you

- The marketing may be non existent.
- You will become an unpaid sales adviser.
- Establishing these companies may be harder.

Identifying the product orientated company

Your initial questioning, at the time of negotiation, must establish whether you are dealing with this type of company. It is suggested that you avoid this type of company in the initial stages of setting up your agencies as it can be frustrating. Later, once you are established, they can be very lucrative in the long term.

The questions to ask:

- How many sales people have they ever had?
- Why did they leave?
- How do they intend to increase sales?
- What is their sales strategy?

The answers given to these questions can usually identify a company that is weak in the selling area. You must always satisfy yourself that the product is saleable.

REDUCING YOUR DISADVANTAGES

You do, of course, have disadvantages over an employed sales-person. Your principal has no control over the actual amount of time that you spend promoting his products or services. How much time you spend on each of your agencies is a matter for you alone to decide. Sometimes a retainer is paid by a principal to get you to spend more time on his business.

A sales agent's disadvantages

- There is no control on time spent on a particular principal's sales.
- The principal cannot discipline you in any way.
- There must be agreement on sales policy.
- The principal must treat you as an independent business.

To reduce the significance of these disadvantages you must concentrate your discussions on the **benefits** of your service.

Retainers and the possible loss of independence

A string usually attached to a retainer is that the principal will usually insist that you spend a set amount of time on his business. What is more they will require you to prove that you spend that time on his business. This will mean unproductive paperwork.

A question that must also be addressed is, what happens when you have accepted a retainer and you find you cannot sell the principal's product or service? He, being an ordinary human being and thinking his offer is the best on the market, will accuse you of not trying and may try to discredit you.

It is, however, unusual for principals to offer retainers. When they do there is usually a reason that must be carefully examined. Have they had a succession of agents and failed to hold them and why are obvious first questions.

Allocating your time

The question of how much time is spent on any one agency causes more anxiety with principals than any other aspect of a sales agent's daily working life. Every principal ideally would like you to spend all your time selling his product or service.

You must be very careful when discussing the amount of your time spent on a principal's behalf and, if needed, diplomatically point out that you have other agencies to represent.

However, you must spread your selling time fairly amongst your agencies. Nothing is worse to a principal than to pay out commission to a sales agent knowing that he is not spending any time on his behalf. As soon as that principal sees an opportunity to appoint a new agent who *will* spend time selling on his behalf, the existing agent will lose that agency.

Be fair to principals:

- Don't 'collect' agencies.
- Give each agency some effort.
- Give up any non producing agency.

WORKING IN TRADITIONAL 'SALES AGENT' INDUSTRIES

There are many industries where the use of sales agents is traditional and has been for many years. Companies that deal direct with retail outlets are probably amongst the largest users of sales agents. The sales agents usually carry a complementary range of products and work to a very tightly scheduled calling pattern on a range of customers, sometimes built up over many years.

Geography also has a bearing on this matter. It is more cost effective to appoint sales agents in the remoter areas of the country, due to the fact that they are covering large areas representing several principals.

It is very easy for people who have experience of calling on retail outlets to make a success of becoming a sales agent in such industries irrespective of whether it is products or services that are offered.

Traditional areas where sales agents operate

- Scotland
- Northern Ireland
- Wales
- South West England

These are all thinly populated areas with long distances between towns.

Traditional industries for sales agents

- Insurance
- Jewellery
- Finance
- Fashion
- Bookselling
- Retail selling

QUESTIONS AND ANSWERS

Q. *I also have to pay myself a salary, pay car expenses, etc. How can I make money where it is uneconomic to pay a salesperson?*

A. You have the advantage that you are spreading those same costs over, perhaps, several agencies and you are selling several products or services to each individual buyer. Your expenses also are tax deductible.

Q. *I am thinking of becoming an agent in a market area where I do not know any buyers. Will this be a disadvantage in obtaining agencies?*

A. A principal, whilst he would prefer people experienced in his industry, will usually make a decision in your favour if you can show him you are good at selling. This includes selling yourself.

Q. *I cannot really see what is wrong with obtaining a retainer. What if several companies offer me a retainer—I can put them all together and make a nice living?*

A. It is unusual for principals to offer retainers. When they do there is usually a reason that must be carefully examined. Have they had a succession of agents and failed to hold them and why are obvious first questions.

CASE STUDIES

Charles sees the way forward

Charles Gann met an old colleague who had become a freelance sales agent some ten years ago. This formerly employed salesman had decided to go freelance after several disappointing jobs. He is now driving an up market car, seemed to be earning a good living and said he was very settled in his way of life. He told Charles of his early efforts to establish himself as a freelance sales agent and told him that initially it was the hardest work he had ever experienced, but being his own boss was a great boost to his self esteem at that time. Now he was established he had principals chasing him to represent them and could afford to be choosy about what agencies he took on.

He gave Charles the names of a couple of companies that he knew were looking for agents and Charles, knowing that he had nothing to lose at this stage, decided to give them a telephone call to find out more about becoming a freelance sales agent.

Dennis is tempted by a retainer

Dennis Wilson saw an advert in a newspaper for self employed salespeople that intimated that very high earnings could be obtained by being successful. The company were offering a retainer for the first six months and there was a company car which had to be paid for out of commission earnings. There was a compulsory 14 day training course with all expenses paid. The whole package was subject to Dennis signing an, as yet unseen, agreement on the first day of the training course.

He was running very short of money and as there were not even any interviews for a paid job in prospect he decided to send in a formal application.

Samantha puts out feelers

Samantha Grey was exploring the possibilities of getting one of her earlier jobs back and spoke to her ex boss. He told her that they did not now employ salespeople directly but that they had a sales agency that did their selling for them. He gave her the name of the person to contact. She also noticed some advertisements in her local paper for what were, in effect, self employed salespeople.

She decided to go down both avenues, rang the sales agency mentioned by her ex boss and wrote off for details of the jobs offered in the adverts.

Discussion points

1. One of the people in our case study is heading for what could be a costly mistake. Can you spot the person and the mistake?

2. Selling the idea of using sales agents may be necessary in some circumstances. What are the major benefits of using agents?

3. Using sales agents also has some disadvantages for a company. Do you know what they are?

3
How to Set Up as a Sales Agent

This chapter will discuss:

- your business plan
- raising finance
- deciding on a working territory
- working from home
- your legal position
- income tax and VAT
- using an accountant.

PREPARING YOUR BUSINESS PLAN

The aim of a business plan and financial forecast is to help you recognise as much as possible what is involved in starting up as a freelance sales agent, from testing its strength as an idea, to assessing your financial needs.

Even if you decide you do not really need financial help, putting the plan before your bank as part of an application for a small overdraft or loan is a good and cheap way of getting a second opinion.

Always be ruthlessly honest in your estimates. Remember, you will pay the price of any mistakes.

Using your bank's standard business plan format
Many banks now provide a blank business plan in the form of a booklet for you to fill in. These are excellent as far as they go but they cover all types of business and can be irrelevant to you in places. In most cases a simple budget, a cash flow forecast and a few answers will be all that is required.

	Jan	Feb	Mar	Apr	May	Jun
Car HP (inc. interest)	250	250	250	250	250	250
Telephone			150			150
Travel expenses	100	100	100	100	100	100
Stationery	250	10	10	10	10	10
Heat & light		60			60	
Postage	10	10	10	10	10	10
Bank charges	20	20	20	20	20	20
Interest	30	30	30	30	30	30
Drawings	1000	1000	1000	1000	1000	1000
Net Debit	1660	1480	1570	1420	1480	1570
Income	1500 (Cash introduced)	100	500	1000	2000	4000
	500 (Loan)					
Credit	340					50
Debit		1040	2110	2900	2380	

Fig. 2. A cashflow forecast.

34

A sales agent's financial affairs are relatively simple in business terms. Do not allow anyone to persuade you otherwise.

For more in-depth information on this subject please read *'How To Manage Budgets and Cashflows'* by Peter Taylor in this series.

A simple example of a cash flow forecast is shown in Figure 2.

Your likely expenditure

The most likely items of initial expenditure are:

- purchase of motor vehicle
- petrol and oil
- vehicle service and repairs
- telephone costs
- stationery and postage
- office furniture
- rent, heat and light
- insurance and national insurance
- secretarial costs
- bank charges
- loan repayments
- drawings against expected profits.

On the matter of drawings, ie wages to yourself, remember that they are 'drawings against expected profit' and you will only be taxed on your total profit including drawings. Try to take out the lowest drawings you can manage initially.

Other charges, such as accountants' costs, will not come in till the second year. Some items listed can be reduced substantially, such as using a computer to cut out secretarial costs and working from home to reduce rent.

Your likely income

The likely income from your efforts is extremely difficult to predict with any certainty. Nevertheless you have to make a forecast. All you can do is add up your total predicted expenditure for the year and that will show the total income you need for the first year without any profit.

This income requirement then can become your total sales forecast for the first year. Do not forget to add the money you are prepared to put in to the business as income, especially if you will be approaching outside finance. They like to see a commitment by you.

The cash flow forecast

Forecasting how the money goes in and out is vital to you and your bank manager. Many items such as telephone bills only occur quarterly. Office furniture and stationery will be paid out at start up. Make a forecast sheet similar to Figure 2 and put the expenditures in as they will occur.

Then add your income. Put any money you propose to add to the business in the first month's income column. The monthly income from commission will be variable and impossible to forecast initially. It is highly likely that the first month's income is nil and will rise from that.

You will have to take your total yearly income forecast and split it into ever increasing monthly amounts. The difference between monthly expenditure and monthly income is your cash flow forecast for that month.

Do not worry about negative cash-flows, ie where expenditure is greater than income, in the initial months. Your bank will expect this. It is the forecast cash-flow at the end of the year that will be relevant.

FINANCE AND WHERE TO GET IT

There are many places to get finance but you will find that the relatively small amounts you may need do restrict your choice.

Sources of finance

- your bank
- finance houses
- various local 'start up' schemes

You will find your local 'Business Link Centre' a source of information on many local 'start up' schemes.

Try to spread the finance by, for instance, funding the vehicle from a hire purchase company and the balance from a bank. Try to avoid giving personal guarantees where possible.

The importance of your presentation

The neat presentation of your proposal is extremely important. If your handwriting or typing is not very good, get your local secretarial bureau to do the layout for you. Get it professionally bound. The local print shop will usually do this for a nominal sum.

DECIDING YOUR WORKING TERRITORY

The area you work in has a vital bearing on your profitability. If you work over too large a territory you will incur extra travel expenses and rob yourself of selling time. The decided area must, however, contain enough potential business and have as many of your existing connections as possible.

Your decision will also be modified by the areas available for the agencies you will be seeking. Do not make the mistake of covering one geographical area for one principal and a different area for another principal. A slight extension of your area to accommodate a principal will not affect your profitability but major extensions will.

WORKING FROM HOME

The majority of agents work from home, at least initially. Try to set a room aside to do your paperwork and telephoning. A certain reasonable percentage of heating, lighting and council tax costs can be set against profits. All office equipment is a tax deductible asset.

Essential office equipment

- telephone
- filing cabinet
- supply of stationery.

As you can see, it does not take much money to start up. To save costs, try buying a second hand filing cabinet.

Optional office equipment

- fax machine

- typewriter or word processing computer
- telephone answering machine.

A word of warning here. If you are new to computers do not buy one at this stage. You will have enough on your hands initially in establishing your agencies. Trying to learn to use a computer at the same time will be distracting.

For further reading on this subject read *How To Work From Home* by Ian Phillipson in this series.

YOUR LEGAL STATUS

When you and your principal agree that you shall become his agent, he is bound by law to honour any agreements to third parties you may make on his behalf. That you made this third party agreement outside your agreement with him is no defence for him. He must honour the agreement as if he made it.

He can, however, try to recoup any losses he has made in such instances from you, if you have acted outside your joint agreement. This rarely happens in practice but does show the protection that can be given by a written agreement.

Under normal circumstances you do not need third party indemnity insurance as an agent.

Forming a limited company

The decision whether to form a limited company is best discussed with your accountant. In the early days it is usually more tax efficient to trade as a 'sole trader' or a 'partnership'. You will also find it easier to obtain finance if you are a sole trader.

Choice of agency name

You can now give your agency any name you wish, apart from copying another company name, without the need to register with Companies House. You must, however, put your own name and the company address on all communications.

The choice of company name should be given some thought. Some agents just use their own name or initials and add the word 'marketing' or 'agent' or similar. Try to avoid too grand a title such as 'Worldwide Systems Ltd' as you will raise prospective customers' expectations too high. Never try to give the impression of what you are not. Low key credibility seems to work best for sales agents.

MANAGING INCOME TAX AND VAT

It is essential that you keep proper records in order to prove your income and outgoings to the relevant tax authority. Even if your system consists of two nails on the wall for bills paid and unpaid and sending them to an accountant at your year end, you must keep records.

The income tax position

Major changes are taking place regarding income tax for the self employed. The system is moving towards 'current year' taxation rather than the previous system where tax was paid in arrears. Class 2 (Self-Employed) National Insurance contributions will also have to be paid monthly.

Basically, at the end of each business year you, or your account-ant, submit your figures to the Inland Revenue and they send you a statement of tax owing. You usually have to pay the tax owing in two payments six months apart. You can appeal against the amount of tax owing.

Failure to submit your figures can lead to your tax being 'assessed'. The assessment figure is usually far higher than the tax involved.

It is suggested that you get in touch with your local Inland Revenue office as soon as you have made the decision to become a freelance sales agent.

The VAT position

Before you start this will need careful consideration. The 'VAT threshold', ie the amount of taxable supplies, or commission invoices in your case, before the need to register for VAT has been increasing of late.

You will have to register for VAT:

● if at the end of any month the value of the taxable supplies, ie commission invoices, you have made in the past 12 months has exceeded £45,000, or

- at any time there are reasonable grounds for believing that the value of taxable supplies you will make in the next 30 days will exceed £45,000.

It is therefore unlikely that you will need to register for VAT initially. When you do need to register, explanatory leaflets are available from your local VAT office.

USING AN ACCOUNTANT

The costs of using an accountant should be recouped by the tax he saves you. Respectable accountants usually have good relations with and are trusted by local Inland Revenue and can act as a buffer for you in any disagreement on taxation.

They can also act as business advisers and will suggest on matters such as finance, tax efficient pensions and many other financial matters. You will probably be charged for this advice so keep your time with him to the minimum.

Doing your own simple bookkeeping will cut down the cost of using an accountant. They charge by the hour. He is then just checking your figures rather than assembling them. There are many simple computer programmes that can do this easily but you can also buy a cheap 'self employed accounts book' that can be filled in and submitted to the accountant.

- Ask other small businessmen for a recommended accountant.
- Make sure he knows what you are trying to achieve.
- Do your bookkeeping at least quarterly.
- Keep every business invoice or docket.
- Submit your figures to him on time.

QUESTIONS AND ANSWERS

Q. *I will find difficulty in estimating my income from commission to put in my budget. How do I do this?*

A. Forecasting is an inexact art. All you can do is calculate your expenditure monthly and this becomes your income target. It is how you progress towards this target that matters.

Q. *My bank will not advance me any finance without me using my house as a guarantee. How do I get round this problem?*
A. Firstly, recalculate your expenditure to see if savings can be made. Then recalculate your expenditure using your credit cards for such items as petrol, stationery etc, thus spreading the credit. You may find you do not need finance.

Q. *Can I reclaim the VAT I pay out even if I am not VAT registered?*
A. No. Only when you are registered is it possible to reclaim VAT.

CASE STUDIES

Charles does it by the book
Charles Gann did his business plan, budget and cash-flow forecast and finds that, by using some of his redundancy money, he does not really need external finance—at least initially. Nevertheless he decides to consult his bank and makes an approach to the small business manager at his local branch (see Figure 3). He has never met him and an appointment is made. He has wisely written his cashflow forecast in such a way as to apparently need a small overdraft at one point which he knows he will not really need and can repay at any time. After consideration the bank agrees his overdraft. They have checked his proposal and found it sound.

Dennis gets into deeper water
Dennis Wilson already has a large overdraft. He is certain his bank will not extend it. He completes his business plan and calculates his financial needs. The major expenditure, a car, was to be paid for out of his commission with the company he is in negotiation with. Nevertheless he will need some money while he is starting up. He sees an advert in the local newspaper for cheap loans and contacts the firm. After a few questions over the phone they send him an application form and a few days later offer to lend him what he wants at a slightly high interest rate and over three years.

Samantha's estimates look promising
Samantha Grey calculates that, providing she gets some commission payments in about three months' time, she can manage

Charles Gann Agencies

(Proprietor: C.H.Gann)

18 Drove Road
Hove
Sussex
BR4 8TH

Mr Alec Harvard, Manager
Anytown Bank Plc
Newtown Rd
Worcester
WR1 7YO

Tel: 01273 678956

6th June 199X

Dear Mr Harvard

I have recently decided to earn my living as a freelance sales agent. As you know, I was made redundant some months ago and my search for new employment had not resulted in a position yet. I feel that I still have a lot to offer as a salesman but I find my age is against me when discussing employment.

This problem does not arise with self employment.

I have already been offered an agency selling similar products to those I sold in my last employment. There are other agencies in prospect.

My business plan shows that I shall need some additional finance during my start up and I would appreciate a discussion with you at your earliest convenience.

To this end I will telephone you on Monday next in the hope that we can meet.

Yours sincerely

Charles Gann

Fig. 3. Letter to bank about a business loan.

easily without outside finance. Her main problem is that the car that she has is getting old and may need some repairs or even replacement, especially with the extra travelling that will be involved with a sales agent's life. She decides to wait to see how her estimated budget works out in practice and then purchase a car through either hire purchase or a personal loan from her bank or her building society.

Discussion points

1. One of the characters has proved the old business saying that the best time to approach a bank for a loan is when you do not need it! Can you spot which character?

2. Why is a small, densely populated area a more profitable proposition for a sales agent?

3. What two forecasts are essential to both you and an outside body when considering finance?

4
Looking for Your First Agencies

In this chapter we will explore:

- looking for agencies
- assessing an agency
- the number of agencies held
- market specialisation
- writing approach letters
- producing a personal profile.

WHERE TO LOOK FOR SALES AGENCIES

There are several places to look for agencies. The *British Agents Register Review* deals exclusively with advertisements for agents. Figure 4 is an example of what you will see on a typical page. Their address is at the end of this book.

Places to look

- The national daily newspapers.
- Local newspapers.
- Your local Job Centre.
- *British Agents Review*.

While you are looking you will also see many 'get rich quick' schemes that sound like agencies. Do not mistake them for genuine sales agent opportunities.

UNIQUE NEW PRODUCT RANGE

- Industrial - Commercial -
- Professional - Governmental -

Established Dynamic Agents Required

High earnings potential with product range which sells to all types of Industry, Commerce, Professions, Authorities - shows massive savings of cash, time and space.

Enormous market/sales potential - already sold in 15 countries worldwide. Commission paid on both new and repeat business.

Professional training and backup for dynamic and ambitious applicants.

IF YOU ARE INTERESTED, CONTACT MR W EVERS

LOEFF'S PATENT (UK) LIMITED

TELEPHONE: 0171-987 1594 . FAX: 0171-987 5932

AUTOMOTIVE BODYSTYLING

and/or

WATERPROOF LEISUREWEAR

We offer you quality products, good commission, marketing and sales backup, friendly and helpful support.

Can you offer us experience and a current customer base in related product areas ?

If so, please contact us at:
Ivra (UK) Limited
IVRA House, 7-8 Barrow Close
Norwich
Norfolk NR3 2AT
Telephone: 01603-482001 (24 hrs)
Fax: 01603-482009

Educational Sales Agents

Commission sales agents required to expand the sales of our specialist educational products throughout the U.K. If you have connections or are currently dealing with primary schools, local authorities and day nurseries, an opportunity now exists for you to join a young and expanding company.

FULL OFFICE SUPPORT PROVIDED. GENEROUS COMMISSION STRUCTURE.

Please write giving details of your experience, products currently sold and the territory in which you operate to:
ALPHA ENDEAVOURS LIMITED
Unit 7, Sidcup Enterprise Centre, Maidstone Road, Sidcup, Kent DA14 5HU

TELEPHONE/FAX: 0181-309 6263

Do you have

contacts

SHOPFITTING
POINT OF SALE
SIGN MAKING
AIRCRAFT INDUSTRIES

Birmingham based company have CNC Routing capacity for machining sheet materials such as MDF, solid wood, plastics, acrylics, aluminium, insulation material, composites etc..The company is also interested in manufacturing complete shopfitting or Point of Sale items such as counter top display units Gondalas etc..

We offer a generous commission and provide contractual exclusivity.

PLEASE CONTACT
DEREK BROWN AT
TOPWOOD (BIRMINGHAM) LTD
ON 0121-384 2393
OR
MIKE EAGLES AT 0121-327 1983

PLUMBING AND BUILDING PRODUCTS

Commission agent required for **North West England, Northern Ireland and the Republic of Ireland** to expand the sales of our repeat consumable brand leaders sold through **Plumbers and Builders Merchants.**

We offer good commission and agency agreement.

Write or fax to: The Managing Director
The Wiseman Group
P.O. Box 58, High Street
Ingatestone, Essex CM4 9DL

BELGIAN CHOCOLATE IMPORTER requires sales agents to sell their luxury range of products into Greeting Card and Gift Shops.

Also well connected agents to sell into Hotel and Catering Trade.

ALL AREAS

Contact:
Mr Oates on 0161-449 7641 day or 0161-456 9682 evening.

Fig. 4. Typical page from the *British Agents Review.*

ASSESSING A GOOD AGENCY

There are no laid down criteria for a good agency. The worth of an agency will depend on your experience and judgement; however, the following points should be addressed.

With a good agency, the product:

- can be sold to your existing contacts
- is competitively priced
- is advertised
- does not conflict with another agency
- has a future
- is already selling
- is readily available
- has good descriptive literature.

Not every agency will offer every one of these points. If any points are non-existent or weak you must decide, on balance, whether you can find a way round these difficulties without compromising an otherwise good potential agency.

HOW MANY AGENCIES SHOULD YOU HOLD?

There is no hard and fast rule here. New agents will find that two in the first year can be handled within their capabilities. With further experience the answer should be, the number of agencies the agent can handle and still give each agency a fair proportion of his time.

There are disturbing numbers of agents who 'collect' agencies in the hope that they will each bring in some unsolicited business without effort on the sales agent's part. Experienced principals, who incidentally tend to offer the best agencies, are aware of such agents and will reject them.

There is a danger in only holding one agency. The Inland Revenue are always seeking examples of tax evasion by people claiming to be self employed but whose efforts are in fact 'controlled' by an employer. Should you hold only one agency for some extended period you may find yourself and your principal investigated.

SPECIALISING IN A MARKET SECTOR

As it is more economic for a sales agent to call on one buyer and sell him several products it is also more efficient to specialise in a market area even if the potential customers are drawn from differing industries. For instance:

- Agency 1. Drinks vending machines
- Agency 2. Snack vending machines
- Agency 3. Vending supplies

calling on:

- offices
- factories
- warehouses
- canteens
- shops.

Market expertise is built up in this way. Most agents choose to operate in a market area that is already known to them. In considering an agency you must ask yourself whether it fits in with your market plan.

WRITING APPROACH LETTERS

Once you have decided to approach a prospective agency you must contact them to arrange a meeting. This can be done by telephone or in writing. If your contact is by telephone you should always confirm the meeting in writing.

An initial letter must always contain enough information to make the principal interested in you but not too much that will allow him to reject you without seeing you.

An initial letter should:

- state where you saw his advertisement
- express your interest
- state your reason for interest
- say briefly why you qualify
- state you are ready for a meeting.

PRODUCING AN AGENCY PROFILE

This is in reality a 'business CV' and is best used at a first meeting with a prospective principal. It must give a professional image and be neatly typed and presented. You are trying to establish your credentials as an independent business person. Your previous CVs were probably trying to establish you as a good employee.

A typical agency profile
A typical profile might contain:

- *header page*
  - the words 'An Agency Profile'
  - the proposed name of your company
  - your business address

- *page 1* your bank address
  - your accountant's address
  - your solicitor's address
  - if applicable, your formation date

- *page 2* the aims of your agency
  - your qualifications to hold the agency
  - any other agencies held
  - third party references

- *page 3* a list of typical customers.

If you are new to being a sales agent do not hide the fact but stress your previous customers even if they are not relevant to the prospective agency. The document should be well spaced and neat and preferably bound.

QUESTIONS AND ANSWERS

Q. *How do I tell genuine agency opportunities from 'get rich quick' schemes?*

A. Generally speaking the 'get rich quick' schemes ask you to pay money in order to gain the agency. Apart from franchises, be wary of any initial monetary involvement.

Q. *Why is an exclusive area important?*
A. Exclusivity means you will get paid a commission on that area *however* the order originates. For example, should your customer telephone his order in, you will still get the commission. Agencies that pay you commission only on the orders you physically get are to be avoided at all costs.

Q. *I am employed as a salesman in an industry that is running down. Should I move into a new industry?*
A. Remember that you will have a learning period if you move. It is probably better to take one agency in your old business in order to retain some income and develop a long term strategy to change industries.

CASE STUDIES

Charles makes progress
Charles Gann was following up the prospective agencies that his ex-colleague had mentioned. He telephoned the sales manager of one and made an appointment for the following week. He could not contact the relevant person of the other company so he decided to write. The letter was brief, to the point and did not say much more than that he understood they were looking for an agent and that he would be interested in discussing this with them. He invited them to telephone him. He also wrote to one of the advertisers in the *British Agents Review* (see Figure 5).

Dennis heads for trouble
Dennis Wilson contacted the company and found that they were offering the retainer for sales agents together with the loan for car purchases. They sent him details which included expensively printed testimonials from sales people stating how working for the company, which made cosmetics and sold them direct to the consumer, had changed their lives. The company booked him on to the next training course and said they would discuss further details with him during this course.

Samantha broadens her horizons
Samantha Grey spoke to the sales manager of the sales agency that was acting on behalf of her previous company. He said that there

Charles Gann Agencies

(Proprietor: C H Gann)

18 Drove Road
Hove
Sussex
BR4 8TH

Tel: 01273 678956

Mr J Monckton, Managing Director
Howard Manufacturing Ltd
Wood End Works
Woodley
Reading
RG3 7YD

6th June 199X

Dear Mr Monckton

Re Agency Advertisement.

I read with interest your advertisement for an agent for the Sussex area in the British Agents Review.

I am about to embark on a career as a sales agent in the Sussex area and have some ten years experience of selling the type of product you mention.

Although this experience has been gained as an employed salesman I am confident that I will be able to sell these products as an agent.

I would be very interested in a meeting in the very near future in order that I might finalise my plans. I can be contacted via the above telephone number at most times.

I look forward to hearing from you.

Yours sincerely

Charles Gann

Fig. 5. Letter responding to an advertisement.

A.B. MARKETING

(Proprietor: S.A.Grey)

Ms Alison Byers, Sales Manager
Gem Cosmetics Ltd
Gemcos House
Tresco Street
Basingstoke
Hants. RG7 8UR

36 Westwood Drive
Sutton Coldfield
W.Mids
B31 7YG

Tel: 0121 403 133655

Dear Ms Byers

I am writing to you to enquire whether you have considered using a sales agent to promote your products in any area?

There are many advantages to you in selling your products through a sales agent; a major benefit, for example, is fixed sales costs. Not needing to administer Income Tax, National Insurance etc is another. I would like to acquaint you with the many other advantages.

I am an experienced, freelance and self employed sales agent calling on retail outlets of the type you supply. At present I am a sales agent for Messrs Quaglotti Perfumes and Cheri Silk Scarves. I have included a short company profile showing my activities with this letter.

I hope we can meet for an initial short discussion on how I think I can improve your sales and your profitability through the use of a sales agent.

To this end I would like to telephone you in about a week's time to gauge your initial reaction and possibly arrange a mutually convenient meeting.

Yours sincerely

Samantha Grey

Fig. 6. Letter prospecting for a possible agency.

A. B. Marketing
An Agency Profile

Formed:	199X	**Bank:**	Anytown Plc High St Branch Sutton Coldfield
Address:	36 Westwood Drive Sutton Coldfield W. Mids B31 7YG		W. Mids.
		Accountants:	Dore & Partners 56 High St Sutton Coldfield W. Mids.
Tel:	0121 403 133655		
		Solicitors:	David Williams & Co.
Proprietor:	Mrs Samantha Grey		169 High St. Sutton Coldfield W. Mids.

Fig. 7. The information contained in a typical agency profile. Ideally this would be spaced out on two or three A4 sheets, with a cover page showing only the agency name.

was a vacancy on the territory that she was interested in and invited her to an interview in about a month's time. She also followed up on the advertisements she had seen and sent them all a letter and agency profile. All the agencies were in different fields but, at this stage, she did not think this would cause a problem.

Discussion points

1. Do you realise the importance of the word 'exclusive' to the territory you will work in and the problems caused by its omission?

2. If you were offered an agency that paid commission to you only when they were paid, would you take it?

3. Why is it important to try to get all your agencies in the same market sector if possible?

Agency aims

The aim of the agency is to capitalise on the market knowledge of the proprietor in the fashion, perfume and cosmetics retail trade. The target geographical areas are the West Midlands and Warwickshire. The proprietor is known to many buyers of these types of products in the area.

It is intended to expand the agency within the next two years. This expansion will come from both expanding the product range and covering a larger geographical area.

It is intended to take on employed salespeople to facilitate this expansion.

Personal history

The proprietor has recently returned to selling after raising a family. Prior to this she was the Sales Manager of Chic Cosmetics having been promoted from an Area Representative.

All her selling life has been spent in the fashion and cosmetics business and she has gained an Open University Degree in Business Studies.

Her family has now grown up leaving sufficient time to follow her career as a freelance sales agent.

Agencies held

Quagliotti Perfumes: Retail perfume sales.
Cheri Silk Scarves: Retail scarf sales.

References

Mr G. Hedron, Man. Direct.   Mrs H. Smithson, Sales Manager
Chic Cosmetics   Fredrickson Fashions
Humber House   Upper Thames St
Victoria St   London
London   SW5 1SS
SW1 3AA

Some typical customers

The Warwick Fashion Group, House of Scott, House of Beautiful Clothes, Dress & Fashion Sense, Country House Perfumes, Occasions, Top Drawer Fashions, The Perfume House, Worcester Perfumerie, Vogue Clothes, Dress Sense, Tiffany Boutique, Reflection Dresses & Fashion, Bon Marche.

5
Selling Yourself to the Principal

This chapter is about:

- choosing a meeting venue
- what the principal wants
- what you must look for
- asking the right questions
- managing the interview
- managing the follow-up.

CHOOSING THE MEETING VENUE

At least one meeting to discuss the agency is inevitable. Try to arrange to visit the principal at his place of work rather than on neutral or your own territory. The reason for this is that there are many subtle signs that can be read if you visit him:

- Are his works or offices run-down?
- Does the telephone ring much while you are there?
- Is there a calm businesslike atmosphere?
- How does he relate to his staff?
- Does the company appear well-established?

The answers to questions such as these can help you make the decision on whether to take the agency.

If you do meet away from his works or offices try to ensure that you can visit them before you finally agree anything.

WHAT THE PRINCIPAL WILL BE LOOKING FOR

The principal will be firstly looking for a good salesperson and secondly for a well connected agent. If this is an attempt to get your first agency, try to get some third-party references to your selling abilities to take to the meeting. Failing this, take a list of the type of customers you already deal with. Do not, of course, leave this list with him.

His first priority is to take on a salesperson who he thinks will be successful for his product or service. You are being interviewed as a salesman rather than an agent at this stage. Before any other matter is discussed you must impress him as a salesperson. The more evidence of this that you can produce the better.

WHAT YOU SHOULD BE LOOKING FOR

At a first meeting you should be looking for:

- a competitive product or service
- reasonable commission
- an agreed, exclusive territory
- acceptable literature and marketing
- sales aids
- advertising and lead generation
- a degree of training
- a formal, written agreement.

These are all basic needs and your own experience will tell you what is acceptable. The formal agreement is dealt with in greater detail in chapter 7.

Other points you must agree

- how and when you will get paid
- what happens with bad debts
- what paperwork do they want
- will they pre-notify any 'house accounts'
- your limits on price negotiation
- who deals with after-sales service.

Making sure you get paid quickly
The most important point here is about getting paid. Never accept a situation where you get your commission only when the customer has paid. You will usually wait a long time.

Agree a bad debt policy
It is quite usual for a principal to deduct from commission owing due to a bad debt. You must jointly agree on the period that will elapse before it is deemed a bad debt.

Minimising paperwork
Paperwork is another potential difficulty. Time spent on paperwork is non-earning time for a sales agent. It is generally accepted that a principal is entitled to a monthly report of your activities on his behalf and any observations on such matters as market trends and competitors' activities. He needs this information to help you in the market. Submitting daily or weekly reports should be diplomatically resisted at all costs.

House accounts agreement
Another area of potential problems is 'house accounts' where the principal has dealt with a customer for a long time and claims that he has gained the business and need not pay a commission on it. It is vital that he declares who these are at the outset. There is nothing worse for an agent than getting orders from a customer only to have the principal claim it as a 'house account' and not pay commission. Another point arises on servicing the 'house accounts': it is unfair to ask an agent to service these accounts without payment.

What are your negotiating limits?
The limits of the agent's authority in dealing with prices or with any other promises made on behalf of the principal must be agreed. The sales agent must know how far he can go in negotiations without reference to the principal.

Who pays for after sales service?
After-sales servicing can be expensive in areas such as machinery sales and many other fields. If it is likely to crop up, agree who is to carry this out and at whose cost before signing the agreement.

ASKING THE RIGHT QUESTIONS

You will find that a checklist of all the above will enable you to ask the right questions. There is nothing worse than leaving an

---

Checklist for the interview

☐	The product	☐	Written agreement
☐	The territory	☐	Termination and duration
☐	Exclusivity	☐	Commission on termination
☐	Commission rate	☐	Compensation or indemnity
☐	Commission due date	☐	Predecessor's reason for leaving
☐	Commission statement	☐	Paperwork and reporting
☐	Bad debt policy	☐	Samples and literature
☐	Negotiation limits	☐	Advertising
☐	Product training	☐	Communications

Fig. 8. The usual questions to ask at an interview.

interview and thinking of unasked questions on important matters.

A list of the most usual questions to ask is shown in Figure 8.

You will find that asking these questions will enhance your credibility with the prospective principal. He will recognise that, even if you are a new sales agent, you know what is involved in running a sales agent's business.

One of the questions is, of course, about what happened to your predecessor. A lot can be revealed about the principal's attitude to agents by the answer to that question.

MANAGING THE INTERVIEW

Due to the unique relationship you will be entering into with the principal, the interview will be rather different to a job interview. You are a potential investor in his business. You are going to invest your time and money in promoting his product or service. You must get this point across at all costs.

The interview will be more balanced than the usual job interview with you wanting to know far more than you would if you were looking for employment. You will, in effect, be interviewing him.

It would not be wise to commit yourself at the first or only interview. There are issues, such as the written agreement, that must be studied before making a final decision. If the principal has not given you a copy of his proposed agreement, ask for a copy to be posted to you and tell him you will give him a decision after you have studied it.

MANAGING THE FOLLOW-UP

After your meeting it is considered polite to write to the principal and thank him for his courtesy and interest. In this letter you should briefly outline any agreements that were jointly reached that you do not expect to be part of the written agreement.

The possibility of extending your area after a trial period is the sort of verbal agreement that will probably not be in the formal agreement. All this will reinforce your professionalism.

QUESTIONS AND ANSWERS

Q. *The principal I am negotiating with is adamant that he will not pay my commission until he gets paid. He is new in the business and says he cannot afford to take the chance of paying commission and not getting paid himself. What do I do?*

A. Explain that you have no objection to repaying the commission should the customer default. Should his fears be based on cash flow problems perhaps you can negotiate an initial period of 'commission on customer payment' and then change to a more normal arrangement. By that time you may have become invaluable to him and you will be in a better negotiating position.

Q. *The principal wants weekly reports of my activities on his behalf and reports on my actions on any sales leads he supplies. Should I agree?*

A. It depends on your assessment of the worth of the agency. You are likely to spend a lot of either your spare time or your selling time servicing his paperwork needs. It is not unusual for principals to request reports on genuine sales leads they supply. They have spent money obtaining them and they wish to judge their effectiveness.

Q. *The principal claims he has some house accounts on the area we are discussing but is avoiding naming them, he says, for commercial reasons. Should I continue negotiating?*

A. Successful agencies are based on mutual trust. Make it a condition of your agreement that he names these accounts should he offer you an agreement. If he refuses you will never be able to have complete trust in him.

CASE STUDIES

Charles finds his first agency

Charles Gann received a telephone call from the managing director of SY Systems, the company he had written to. He invited Charles to a meeting the following week at his offices. This meant he now had two appointments to discuss agencies. At the meeting with SY Systems he was most impressed with the way the company seemed to be run and he was shown the products. He was sure he could sell them to his old customers.

Charles showed the MD the company profile he had prepared. They went through it together and the MD remarked that he noticed that Charles had not got any agency experience. Charles countered by saying that though he was not an experienced agent he had all the right attributes, namely, sales experience, a customer base and enough money to tide him over until he was established. He told the MD that he intended to take on other, non competing, agencies.

The MD accepted this and said that, at this stage, he was quite prepared to offer Charles the agency in writing. Charles asked that a copy of the written agreement be sent to him for his comment. This was agreed.

Dennis gets into deep water

Dennis Wilson attended the training course at a nearby hotel but found he was not really required to sell himself to the principal. In fact the major problem was to identify who was in charge. The days were taken up by very professional presentations and videos by various members of the company's executives. At no time did anyone discuss his sales experience or personal circumstances.

He found out that he was expected to pay for his samples and literature. He also found that his commission rate was weighted in such a way that he had to find other salespeople to earn maximum commission. The company offered to lend him the money for his samples together with the loan for the car and deduct it from his future commission.

The training course ran late and ended in a hurry with no chance for Dennis to talk to anyone about the fact that he still had not received an agreement despite several phone calls and letters to the sales manager (see Figure 9). He was then told that the folder he had been given contained two copies of the agreement and would he sign it and return one copy of the company?

Samantha hears warning bells

Samantha Grey attended the interview offered to her by the sales agency. She was rather shocked to find that the offices were rather dirty, the sales director was late for the appointment and during the appointment the telephone rang many times. He apologised and left the room to answer the calls each time. He seemed flustered each time he returned.

Without even reading Samantha's expensively produced company profile he offered Samantha the agency. The commission rates seemed extremely good and far better than she had expected. She was told that new literature was being prepared and that they had run out of the existing literature so she could not take any away to look at.

The written agreement would be put in the post to her and a start date was mentioned but Samantha, wisely, said she wanted time.

In the meantime she had attended a much more positive

DENNIS WILSON

45 Newsome Gardens
Sutton
Surrey
GU17 7UJ

Eastern Products Ltd
123 Great Eastern Way
Great Dunmow
Essex
CT13 6YH

Tel: 01643 76954

4th February 199X

For the attention of Mr Greg Harris. Sales Manager.

Dear Greg

Further to our recent meetings and my verbal acceptance of the agency for the Surrey and Sussex areas, I still have not received the promised written agreement from you despite several promises from you.

As you know, a written agreement protects both parties and proceeding on a verbal basis can lead to mis-understandings. I am keen to bring your products to the attention of my customers where I think they will sell extremely well.

I do not wish to jeopardise this potential for both of us by letting mis-understandings creep in.

If I do not receive at least a draft agreement from you by the end of the month, regretfully I will not feel able to take up your kind offer of an agency.

This would be a pity, due to the work both of us have put in so far and the loss of potential sales from my customers.

I look forward to hearing from you.

Yours truly

Dennis Wilson

Fig. 9. Letter about lack of an agency agreement.

A.B. MARKETING

(Proprietor: S.A.Grey)

36 Westwood Drive
Sutton Coldfield
W.Mids
B31 7YG

Ms Alison Byers, Sales Manager
Gem Cosmetics Ltd
Gemcos House
Tresco Street
Basingstoke
Hants. RG7 8UR

Tel: 0121 403 133655

20th June 199X

Dear Alison

Many thanks for our meeting yesterday and your very interesting tour of your works. I think your company has an excellent product range and the marketing skills to match.

At this stage I would be very pleased to work with you and I am confident that I can increase sales on the area we spoke of. I am also pleased that you appreciated the role of a sales agent even though you have only used employed people before.

There is the matter of the written Agency Agreement to be drawn up and agreed. Perhaps we can work together on this before you involve your legal advisors in order that we might avoid the inevitable amendments that are produced if they draw up the first draft.

For your information, the British Agents Register produce an excellent booklet on agency agreements, including the EC Directive that we discussed. This booklet provides a good starting point for an agreement. If you would care to telephone me I will give you the address.

I look forward to our meeting with your Managing Director on the 30th June.

Yours truly

Samantha Grey

Fig. 10. Follow up letter after an interview.

interview with one of the advertisers whom she had approached. During this interview the question of an agreement had been raised, and it became apparent that the interviewer was unaware of the existence of the EC directive on agency agreements (see chapter 6). Samantha decided to use her follow-up letter to explore the issue (see Figure 10).

Discussion points
1. Why is it important that 'House Accounts' are agreed before anything is signed?

2. Why should paperwork be kept to the minimum?

3. What are your attitudes to collecting outstanding monies on behalf of your principal?

6
Negotiating the Formal Agreement

This chapter looks at:

- the need for a formal agreement
- the EC directive on agency agreements
- the elements of the agreement
- what to do if the agreement is breached.

REQUESTING AN AGREEMENT

A written agreement should be considered a necessity with any agency. When it is jointly signed it should be put away for safekeeping and hopefully never consulted again. It is a sign that something has gone wrong with your relationship if you are viewing your agreement regularly.

Some agents have held agencies for many years based on little more than a handshake and goodwill. In today's business world this is a risky situation. Early in your negotiations ask for a written agreement and view any reluctance to provide this with suspicion.

THE EC DIRECTIVE ON COMMERCIAL AGENTS' AGREEMENTS

A European Council directive on agency agreements standardises some parts of such agreements across the whole of the EU. It also gives the force of law to these clauses whether there is a written agreement or not. An outline of the directive is laid out in appendix 1.

This is the first recognition of the legal status of a commercial agent in UK civil law. In the past, the standing of the written agreement was based on the law of contract. This law has many interpretations and does not specifically deal with agents. Nevertheless, the EC directive contains many clauses such as 'reasonable' and 'good faith' which have yet to be tested in the UK courts.

Many principals with existing agreements have tried and are trying to find ways round this legislation mainly due to its provision for compensation or indemnity owing to the agent on the ending of the agency. One way is to actually employ the agent but only pay him a commission on sales. This, of course, destroys the self-employed status of the agent with its advantages to both parties.

As a new agent you should not come across this problem.

THE ELEMENTS OF THE AGREEMENT

The written agreement should deal with the following points:

- the geographical area or type of customer
- exclusivity of area of operation
- commission rates and when payable
- the products
- termination of the agreement
- supply of sales aids
- the negotiation limits
- what house accounts there are
- paperwork requirements
- notification of orders placed direct.

The negotiable clauses

All these points are negotiable, of course. Some principals who have an existing team of agents may not wish to vary their existing agreement. Although specific mention of the EC directive may not be made in the agreement, the directive states that the regulations shall apply to all agreements made after 1 January 1994.

IF THE AGREEMENT IS BREACHED

All agreements, in reality, rely mainly on trust and goodwill between two parties. The alternative is costly legal argument.

There are as many unwritten rules in the relationship as there are clauses in the written agreement. Try to foster an open and honest attitude to your principal.

The first rule, if a breach of agreement becomes obvious to either party, is not to go to law immediately. If you think the agreement has been breached by the principal meet him to discuss it. In many cases it will be a pure oversight on his part and he will rectify it and apologise.

If the breach seems deliberate, again meet him to voice your point of view and then confirm your points in writing. Should he not be moved into rectifying the situation you then have a decision to make. Do you resort to the law or do you carry out the ultimate sanction and withdraw from the agreement and take your customers with you?

Each individual case will vary and this is a decision that you alone can take. It must be borne in mind that your relationship has broken down and that no amount of legal procedures will put it together again. If it is a monetary matter the amount you could lose through legal action should be taken into account.

QUESTIONS AND ANSWERS

Q. *The principal says he knows nothing of the EC Directive on Agency Agreements and wants nothing to do with it. Do I go on negotiating?*

A. Do let him know that the clauses in the directive have the force of law and override any similar clauses in any written agreement. The clauses also have the force of law whether there is a written agreement or not. The directive does not contain any measures that could not be expected in an agreement between two equal and honourable parties.

Q. *There are other agents working for the principal on the area we are talking about. Should I sign the agreement?*

A. Do not sign the agreement until you have established an area as exclusive to you. Whether this area is geographical or market based is up to the individual circumstances. You could find the results of your efforts going to someone else's pocket including the principal's.

Q. *The sales aids provided are very expensive and the principal wants me to pay for them. Do I buy them?*

A. As a general rule no. Offer to give him a deposit on them if he is insistent. The question arises as to what happens when the sales aids need renewing or a new model or service is launched.

CASE STUDIES

Charles reads the small print

Charles Gann received the formal agreement in the post a couple of days later. He checked it against what was said at the meeting. He also checked it against the EC directive on agency agreements and noticed that there were no references to either compensation or indemnity should they decide to dispense with his services at some time in the future.

He also noticed that the time scale of the notice period was one month for both parties throughout the life of the agreement. This did not match the EC directive that had a sliding scale dictating up to a maximum three months' notice after the commencement of the third year of the agreement.

Charles rang the principal who apologised and said that they did know there was an EC directive but did not know what was in it. They said they would match anything in the directive and promised to consult their solicitor and send him a new agreement.

Dennis's agreement is full of holes

Dennis Wilson read the agreement he was given on the training course. He noticed that there was no exclusivity on the area and that the company reserved the right to appoint other agents on his area at their own discretion. He also noticed that, even though the loan for the car and samples were mentioned, no interest rate was specified. He wished he had clarified this point on the training course but he remembered they had not given him time.

He contacted them but had difficulty in finding the right person. When he eventually spoke to the sales manager, whom he had not met, he said that they would not take on any other sales agent for his area and that clause in the agreement was a safety measure on the company's part.

Regarding the interest on the loan for the car and samples, this would be at a floating rate. Dennis had to break off the conversation because his new car had just arrived.

Samantha encounters a delay

Samantha Grey waited a couple of weeks and, not having received the promised agreement, telephoned the sales director. He said that they had given the matter some thought and that, due to a report from their solicitor on the effect of the EC directive, they were postponing sending the agreement to her. They still wanted her to start as an agent. She said she would not start without a formal agreement being signed.

Samantha was getting worried about the time it was taking and decided to chase up some of the other agencies she had applied for. A couple of telephone calls soom established that both the companies were still actively looking for agents and had not contacted her for what seemed perfectly valid reasons.

Discussion points

1. What would you do if an intended principal said he wanted nothing to do with the terms that were in the EC Directive on Agency Agreements?

2. How can agreeing your negotiating limits with your principal affect your credibility with your customers?

3. Do you think an area should always be based on geographical limits or can it be based on certain specified industries?

7
Carrying Out Checks on the Principal

Things to do after the interview are:

- a bank credit check
- checking via a credit investigation agency
- using your local library
- identifying a risky principal
- speak to his existing agents.

It is obvious that if you take on an agency with an unsound principal your investment in time, travel and incidental expenses will be at risk. All steps should be taken to ensure that you are acting for a company that can and will deliver the goods or service and pay your commission on time.

CHECKING WITH YOUR BANK

This is one of the easiest checks to make but it will tell you little apart from his bank's assessment of his creditworthiness at the time of asking. You will need to tell your bank his bank's address and his correct trading title. Ask him for this information during your first interview. It should demonstrate to him your caution in money matters. You will also have to let your bank know how much you think he will owe you at any one time. This will have to be a guess on your part.

The answer from your bank will be couched in bankers' terms and will probably say something like 'ABCD is good for the amount stated'. This does not tell you a lot as his bank would hardly advertise the fact that they think his business is risky and thereby affect his trading.

USING A CREDIT INFORMATION AGENCY

There are many credit investigation companies who will give you a far more independent assessment of the company you are intending to take an agency with. Their assessment is based on other companies' actual trading experience. Many credit investigation companies are listed in the *Yellow Pages*. You will have to pay for these services.

USING YOUR LOCAL LIBRARY

A lot of information can be gleaned from the reference section of your local library. Publications such as *Krones Guide* and *Kompass* list most registered companies, their directors and recent profits. It is as well to check with these to confirm what you were told during the interview.

IDENTIFYING A RISKY PRINCIPAL

This is a most difficult thing to do. Apart from the credit checks mentioned, if you are staying in the industry you previously sold in, ask your customers about your prospective principal. It is amazing how risky companies draw attention to themselves.

Possible signs of a risky principal

- late deliveries
- undue debt chasing
- regular and large discounting
- recent name changes
- stock shortages
- high staff turnover
- extravagant product claims
- will not name satisfied customers.

The main aim is to keep your eyes and ears open. Constantly watch for the signs and be prepared to act on them.

SPEAK TO HIS EXISTING AGENTS

At the interview ask him for the name and telephone number of a couple of his existing sales agents and telephone them. Usually they will give you an honest assessment of the principal from the agent's point of view. They are not employed by him so they have no need to give a dishonest answer.

QUESTIONS AND ANSWERS

Q. *Being already in the same business as my prospective agency I asked one of my customers about the principal and he was most uncomplimentary. Should I pull out of negotiations?*

A. Make further investigations and if you receive similar answers from other customers go carefully. Do not take the first customer's views in isolation. The problem may have been caused by the customer.

Q. *It is obvious that the principal has had a high turnover of agents recently. How can I find out the reason?*

A. Some detective work is called for. Through a third party, try to find the name and telephone number of one of his agents, either past or present, and contact the agent. You must take whatever is said on its face value and use it as background knowledge.

Q. *I do not believe the claims that the principal is making about his product. How do I check?*

A. Take a guess on who his customers should be and telephone to ask them politely, what they think of the product. Bad news travels fast. They will soon tell you if the product is not as good as is claimed.

CASE STUDIES

Charles takes the plunge

Charles Gann was waiting for the new written agreement to arrive and used this time to do some credit checks on the principal. He wrote to his bank quoting the bank details he had been given and told them how much he expected to be invoicing them monthly. He received a reply some ten days later that said that they were 'a well run company who would not enter into debts they could not service'.

Charles thought that this was a bit vague and decided to contact a credit checking agency that he found in the *Yellow Pages*. He telephoned them and they told him that if he wrote, enclosed all the details and a cheque for £20, they would give him a credit rating for the company. He did this and received a reply by return of post that was a complete breakdown of the company's financial affairs going back some five years and a credit rating that far exceeded the figure that he had in mind.

He felt completely happy with the financial stability of the company. He also received the new written agreement, checked it and could not find any major problems.

He telephoned the principal and told him he was going to sign the agreement and they arranged a starting date.

Dennis gets into more trouble

Dennis Wilson was having one of his regular meetings with his bank manager about his overdraft. He updated the manager with his negotiations so far. The bank manager suggested that he ought to make a credit check on the company and offered to do it on his behalf if he could send him the details. Dennis agreed. He tried various persons within the company but could not get anyone to give him the details he wanted.

The sales director of the company telephoned to say that he wanted Dennis to start selling on their behalf next week. Dennis told him that he still was not satisfied with the agreement as it stood but the sales director said they could sort the matter out afterwards.

Dennis decided to go ahead and start as he was desperately short of money.

Samantha plays safe

Samantha Grey received a letter from the company saying that they could not change the agreement to fall in line with the EC Directive but they would like her to start selling for them using their standard agreement. Samantha did not commit herself and gave them some excuses why she could not sign and start selling for them yet.

She had interviews with the other two companies and they both came up to the criteria she had set. They both meant calling on the same customers, the commissions were adequate and the written agreements, although slightly different, were to her satisfaction.

She accepted both the agencies and wrote a polite letter to the first agency declining their offer. She arranged a starting date for both.

Discussion points

1. Why is it important to check the creditworthiness of a potential principal?

2. Would you always accept any 'third party' view on the principal's creditworthiness?

3. Do you know some of the signs that would suggest a lack of creditworthiness other than bank checks, etc?

8
Running Your Agency

Major factors in running your agency are:

- buying and running a car
- using a computer
- invoicing and chasing commission
- managing your finances
- communication with your principals
- journey planning.

BUYING AND RUNNING A CAR

This is an area of your operation that needs great thought. A vehicle that constantly lets you down can affect your earnings. For example, lateness or cancellation of appointments can affect your credibility with your customers. On the other hand an expensive, up-market car with high running costs could sink your agency in its initial stages. It is better to wait till you can afford the expensive car you always wanted.

Many agents run, and can afford to run, far more expensive cars than their employed counterparts but they usually waited till they could afford it. Even if you are used to having the latest model of an executive saloon, supplied by your employer of course, do not be afraid of being seen in a clean, well maintained second hand car.

You cannot use a normal car insurance policy. Insurance companies consider you are a 'commercial traveller' and you must have a special insurance policy. These policies are more expensive but you must avoid saving money by using a normal policy. If you have an accident whilst you are using the vehicle at work you are not insured.

Ways of financing a vehicle

There are many ways of financing the purchase of a car and your choice will be dictated by your circumstances. In the initial stages it is wiser to try to avoid long term and heavy financial commitments.

Vehicles can be financed by:

- hire purchase
- hire purchase with buy back
- long term lease
- lease purchase
- bank loan
- building society loan
- outright purchase.

If you are being made redundant by your company it may be possible to arrange to take over the car you are driving at present, always assuming it is in good condition.

USING A COMPUTER

A computer is, without doubt, a most useful tool for a busy agent. It can, after the initial learning period, save many hours of valuable selling and spare time in automating your administration. Using its word processing facilities can also save secretarial fees.

Computers can be used for:

- book-keeping
- VAT returns
- letter writing
- mailshots
- customer lists
- performance analysis.

If you are new to computers try to avoid buying one until you feel established as an agent. Computers are very absorbing and annoying machines. Much time can be spent on learning to run them when you should be out selling face to face with customers. Once you are established and use a computer they become indispensable.

There is a lot of technical jargon used in connection with computers. Do not be put off by this. It is quite possible to run a computer without becoming a computer buff. For example the jargon words 'hardware' and 'software' baffles many non computer users. Hardware is the actual computer and its accessories such as printers, software is the programmes that run on them.

Choosing the hardware

Beware of going in to your local computer shop and asking the salesperson which is the best computer for you. This is like asking a crocodile where to swim. Ask any computer-literate friend or acquaintance to help you. There are many evening classes run by local colleges that run computer classes. Joining one of these will teach you more about computers and will help you make a choice based on your own experiences.

Always buy a machine that can be up-graded later. Things are moving fast in the computer industry. What is considered state of the art today becomes obsolete in a couple of years' time. There is no need to become a slave to the latest fads in computers but it is useful to be able to run the latest software if it will increase your efficiency and save you time.

Choosing the software

The advent of such software programs as 'Windows' brings the whole operation down, basically, to using a movable 'mouse' to move a cursor to an area of the screen with the 'action button' or 'Menu' that you want to activate and clicking with the 'mouse button'.

The software one might need includes:

- word processing
- simple accounts
- database
- spreadsheet.

There are some excellent, so called 'integrated' packages on the market that contain all these programmes that link together. They will enable you to do such things as using the word processing software to prepare a mailshot then address the mailshot to

Screenshots from Money Manager Business Edition

```
                        Business data sample
                 Monthly Class Totals for Jan-94 to Dec-94
                 Apr   May   Jun   Jul   Aug   Sep   Oct   Nov   Dec  YEAR
OVERHEADS                                                                  0
Wages           500-  500-  500-  500-  500-  500-  500-  500-  500- 6000-
Rent            360-  360-  360-  360-  360-  360-  360-  360-  360- 4320-
Utilities             45-                            33-         26-   139-
Telephone       156-              89-                     296-        773-
Postage               36-   44-   23-   44-   66-   56-   23-   67-   472-
Stationery      22-   9-    22-   31-   16-         56-   10-   12-   350-
Travel          139-  74-   176-  67-   82-   43-   82-         55-   97- 1342-
MARKETING                                                                  0
Advertising     346-        692-  346-  346-  346-  372-  372-  372- 4231-
Printing                                            233-             233-
PRODUCTION                                                                 0
Raw materials         375-  409-  78-   185-  141-  172-  149-  220- 2412-
Packaging       0-    211-  55-         13-   26-   15-         46-   441-
TRANSFERS                                                             2000
Receipts                                                             2000
End Balance    31258 34567 35528 36593 36959 37433 37407 37994 40402 40402
Income          6578  7734  5514  4636  4146  4306  4009  4154  8592 73636
Outgoings      4570- 4425- 4554- 3571- 3780- 3831- 4036- 3567- 6184-61731-
Cash flow       2008  3309   961  1065   366   474   27-   587  2408 11906
↑   Report completed ... press Esc to continue, P to print, F for file
```

```
Account codes:                                          27 entries
b Nat West      c Cash       v UAT        p Purchases
r Bus Reserve   a Access     s Sales
Class codes:
s0 SALES       fu UAT       ow Wages      oc Travel     pm Raw material
sg Goods       a0 CAPITAL EQUI or Rent    om Misc.      pp Packaging
ss Services    ac Cars      ou Utilities  m0 MARKETING  x0 TRANSFERS
dd DRAWINGS    a0 Office equip ot Telephone ma Advertising xp Payments
f0 FINANCIAL   am Machinery  op Postage    mp Printing   xr Receipts
fc Chrgs & int o0 OVERHEADS  os Stationery p0 PRODUCTION
   Jan Feb Mar Apr May Jun Jul Aug Sep Oct Nov Dec
Day Ref  Ac S-Ac Cl Description      Rec    Debit  Credit  UAT
  1  so       b   or Rent            y     360.00
  1          r   . fc Chrgs & int    y             144.20  x
  1          r     fc Chrgs & int    y     117.50          s
  1 121      c     oc Travel               18.37           s
  1 122    p acme  pm Raw materials        220.47          s
  1 so       b     dd DRAWINGS       y    1500.00          x
  3 123      c     oc Travel               20.00           s
                   Train to Derby
  4 124    s lswl  sg Goods                        932.00  s
  7 so       b     ss Archer & Co.   y             180.00  s
  9 125      c  .  os Stationery              5.45         s
  9 126      a     oc Travel         y       19.48         s
 11 127    s lswl  sg Goods                        1292.01 s
```

Fig. 11. Examples from 'Money Manager' accounts software.

customers drawn from the database program. These integrated programmes are quite adequate for your likely initial and possibly, long term, use.

A simple accounts package is shown in Figure 11. This package is called Money Manager. The address of the seller is in the useful addresses section of this book. It is inexpensive, simple and has the major advantage that it can be easily understood by someone with no accounts experience. Mistakes can be rectified easily which cannot be said of many accounts software.

Further reading is contained in 'How to Manage Computers at Work' by Graham Jones in this series.

INVOICING AND CHASING YOUR COMMISSION

One of the most important and satisfying aspects of your agency is invoicing your commission. Some of your principals may be in

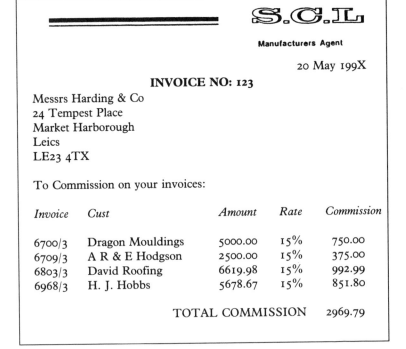

S.C.L

Manufacturers Agent

20 May 199X

INVOICE NO: 123

Messrs Harding & Co
24 Tempest Place
Market Harborough
Leics
LE23 4TX

To Commission on your invoices:

Invoice	Cust	Amount	Rate	Commission
6700/3	Dragon Mouldings	5000.00	15%	750.00
6709/3	A R & E Hodgson	2500.00	15%	375.00
6803/3	David Roofing	6619.98	15%	992.99
6968/3	H. J. Hobbs	5678.67	15%	851.80
	TOTAL COMMISSION			2969.79

Fig. 12. A typical agent's invoice

a 'self-billing scheme' for VAT purposes and you may not need to invoice them, but the majority will need an invoice from you. These invoices can be simply typed out on your own letterheaded notepaper.

Always keep a record of orders placed through yourself. Your written agreement should have provided that the principal notifies you of all orders that are placed direct with him on your area and are commissionable. This normally means a monthly statement from him that you check and invoice accordingly.

When the commission is due depends on your agreement with the principal. A usual arrangement is at the month end following the month of invoice. A typical agent's invoice is shown in Figure 12.

Chasing your commission

Never fail to chase any late payment of a commission invoice. Politely point out to your principal that your invoices are both wages and expenses to you. Should he pay the wages and expenses of his employees late he would soon find himself looking for new employees. You are no exception.

MANAGING YOUR FINANCES

We dealt with budgeting and cashflow forecasting in an earlier chapter. It is vital that you monitor your progress towards these targets on a regular basis. Do not make this an obsession but do spend a half hour or so a month checking your progress. If you are running into financial problems, the earlier you spot it the earlier you can take remedial action.

Paying your bills is another matter that has to be attended to regularly. Try to arrange a set time in the month to receive your bank statement and, at that time, sit down and plan what bills you have to pay and what income you will have to pay them.

A simple idea is to have two files, one for bills yet to be paid and one for those already paid. Monthly action on the bills 'yet to be paid file' will keep you in your suppliers' good books. If you find your cashflow will not allow you to pay some bills, pay part of them and contact the suppliers and give them an estimate of when you can pay the balance and stick to that estimate. Do not ignore bills you cannot pay.

DENNIS WILSON
45 Newsome Gardens
Sutton
Surrey
GU17 7UJ

Tel: 01643 76954

Eastern Products Ltd
123 Gt Eastern Way
Great Dunmow
Essex
CT13 6YH

6th June 199X

For the attention of Greg Harris, Sales Manager.

Dear Greg

Annual Holidays 199X

The writer will not be on his territory from Monday 14th July to Monday 21st July inclusive.

There is an outstanding problem regarding the delivery to Gemini that may arise while I am absent. Could you please deal with this if it does arise?

I have notified all my existing customers. Those that normally place orders direct with me have promised to place them direct with you.

There should be a considerable order from Harrisons during my absence. If it fails to arrive by about the 17th, could you telephone Fred George and give him a polite reminder?

If there are any other messages could you please hold them until my return.

Best regards

Dennis Wilson

Fig. 13. Letter to principal about absence from territory.

Agents Name....JAMES   Area No...10.   Month...MAY.9X

CUSTOMER	Potential Order	Product	Comments
BLOGGS + CO	£5,000	DSP	WILL ORDER JUNE
SMITH + HARRIS	£2,000	EL608	PROJECT CANCELLED
JONES CONTRACTORS	£7,000	CRC	PLACED ORDER
SHILMAN + WRIGHT	£650	CWC	ORDER JULY.

Fig. 14. A typical agent's monthly report.

Another way of spreading the finances is to pay as much as possible by credit card. This means that, should you be in a lean period, you can pay the minimum amount and then completely clear your debt when you have a good month. Beware building up a large debt on your credit cards due to the relatively high interest rates.

COMMUNICATION WITH YOUR PRINCIPALS

It is vital that you keep in touch with your principals on a regular basis. They want to know what is going on in your area. There is nothing worse to a principal than not to hear from an agent for weeks or even months. He automatically assumes you are not promoting his product. You may be working extremely hard on his behalf but lack of contact can, quite mistakenly, lead to him thinking the worst.

You must always, as a matter of courtesy and efficiency, let all your principals know if you are going on holiday, are off work sick or are absent for any other reason.

Even if you are failing to get orders for him, contact him and discuss ways that you can jointly increase the business.

Figure 13 shows a letter from Dennis Wilson to one of his principals informing him of a forthcoming absence.

Submitting monthly reports

Any business-like principal will ask you for a monthly report of the activity on your area. It is sometimes a bit irksome but do remember he has to plan his production or stock levels or finances on market information. Your estimate of market trends, orders in the pipeline and in negotiation, together with the estimates from his other agents, can give him the information he needs to help you.

You may be disinclined to go into too much detail about your contacts, but a general outline should suffice. It is usually sufficient to say that you are expecting an order worth £500 from XYZ Ltd rather than you are dealing with Fred Bloggs of XYZ Ltd. An example of a monthly report is shown in Figure 14.

It is wise to resist any attempt by the principal to get you to report on a daily or weekly basis. However, reports on special projects he may initiate are quite in order. He is trying to help you, you must try to help him.

THE IMPORTANCE OF JOURNEY PLANNING

This is a phrase that often crops up with regard to paid salespeople and is often given little attention. Now that you will be paying the travelling expenses it does become extremely important. It is beyond the scope of this book to discuss journey planning, any good salesperson will know the basics. Trying to keep to an efficient journey plan has a two-fold benefit to you: it maximises your selling time and decreases your expenses.

Making appointments

The importance of making appointments for every call depends on the industry you work in. In retail selling it is less important than being expected at a certain time of the month by your regular customers and making appointments to see new prospects. In selling capital goods such as machinery etc, appointments are vital.

Try and set a fixed time every week to telephone for appointments with new prospects. The knowledge that the person you want to speak to is actually there when you visit is a financial consideration for an agent.

QUESTIONS AND ANSWERS

Q. *I have seen some second hand computers advertised. Should I consider buying one?*

A. There are some excellent bargains to be had second hand. Always take some one who knows something about computers with you to view them and always insist on seeing it running.

Q. *The principal says he cannot send me a statement of commission earned every month and that I will have to claim the commission earned. What is the danger in this?*

A. The danger here is that you have no record of any orders that your customer has placed direct with him. If he were dishonourable he could pocket the commission on these orders without you knowing. For a time!

Q. *How often should I communicate with a principal?*

A. There is no hard and fast rule here. In an active business relationship once a week is not too often. Once a month would tend to put a strain on the relationship.

CASE STUDIES

Charles decides on a HP car

Charles Gann started looking for a car. He decided he would go for a low-mileage, second hand executive model. He thought they represented excellent value for money as the 'write down', meaning the drop in value from new to second hand, on this type of vehicle is high. He visited a vehicle leasing company who were selling some of their ex-lease cars and found an excellent car some three years old with high mileage but well maintained,

DENNIS WILSON

45 Newsome Gardens
Sutton
Surrey
GU17 7UJ

Eastern Products Ltd
123 Great Eastern Way
Great Dunmow
Essex
CT13 6YH

Tel: 01643 76954

14th July 199X

For the attention of Mr Greg Harris, Sales Manager.

Dear Greg

    Re: Commission Invoice 56345, £945.87, 1/4/9X

Despite several telephone calls to the Mrs Gregson of your Financial Dept, my invoice for my March commission still remains unpaid.

Mrs Gregson stated that there were no problems with the calculations in the invoice.

I am sure that you understand that my commission invoice represents both salary and expenses for me and that I have already had to pay for items such as petrol, telephone etc. In the absence of payment I have to borrow this money which, of course, incurs interest.

I would be grateful if you could intervene and expedite payment.

Could you telephone me and inform me when I might receive payment?

Yours truly

Dennis Wilson

Fig. 15. Letter chasing commission payment.

He arranged hire purchase through the leasing company. He could have purchased the car outright but felt he would like to retain as much financial reserve as he could. If things went well he could always pay the hire purchase off early and save interest payment. He made sure that there were minimum early payment penalties in the HP agreement.

Dennis realises his mistake

Dennis Wilson was already equipped with a new car, to be paid for by deductions from his commissions. He was now ready to go out selling. He was keen to be earning because his bank were chasing him hard to reduce his overdraft.

Dennis started telephoning potential customers and found that he was very coldly received and, after having spent a couple of days on the telephone, he had managed to obtain only two appointments. He was a bit annoyed by a telephone call from his principal at the end of the first week asking him for a breakdown of his appointments for the following week. There was a form to fill in and, even though he was slightly uneasy about it, he filled it in.

Over the next few weeks Dennis found himself spending most of his time on the telephone trying to get appointments. He did get some but the ratio was about ten phone calls to one appointment. When fulfilling the appointments with the prospective customers he found that they found every excuse not to buy the product.

Dennis started to realise that he had made a bad choice of either principal or product but he was committed to paying for his car and samples. He also found, when his hard-won orders did start to come through, that his commission was very slow to follow (see Figure 15).

Samantha gets good news

Samantha Grey was using the car that she already owned so that was one decision she did not have to make. She decided that she would buy a computer, mainly for its word processing capability. She was not very good at typing and wanted to do lots of mailshots herself to save the costs of using a secretarial bureau.

She had budgeted for this item together with the other things she needed such as an office desk, a telephone answering machine and all the other items that are found in an efficient and modern office.

It was while she was connecting the computer up that she received a telephone call from one of her new principals telling her that an interested potential customer had telephoned them asking to see someone about their offer. Could she telephone the customer and take the appointment? Samantha was on the way to making her first commission cheque.

Discussion points

1. Why is it so important to invoice your commission promptly?

2. How often would you check your actual expenditure against your budgeted expenditure?

3. In the case studies Dennis Wilson is running into major problems. What do you think is the primary cause of these problems?

9
Developing Your Customer Base

This chapter is about:

- cultivating an independent role
- keeping your customers informed
- promoting your complete range
- helping your principal get paid
- keeping promises
- dealing with complaints.

THE AGENT'S INDEPENDENT ROLE

As an agent you must do all you can to stress your independence. Most buyers in the UK are used to being called on mainly by employed salespeople and, if not told otherwise, will see you in the same light. They expect employed salespeople to give them a biased view. They make their assessments on this view.

Find every opportunity to reinforce your role as an adviser rather than a salesperson. A useful tactic is to tell him of your other agencies, even if they are of no interest to him as a buyer. Always say 'they' rather than 'we' when talking to him about any of the agencies you hold. Always be ready to take the customer's side, assuming he is correct, in any dispute with your principal. Remember they are your customers! They are your main asset.

It is quite usual to find agents who hold their customers in greater regard than their principals. As with many things it is a matter of balance.

KEEPING YOUR CUSTOMERS INFORMED

This is an important feature of your life as a sales agent. Do not leave it to each principal to decide whether to inform your customers of the latest developments in his range. If necessary prompt him. An agent should possibly do this himself, if only to reinforce his role as an adviser.

Some ways of informing customers are:

- calling on them
- telephoning them
- newsletters
- mailshots from principals
- mailshots from the agent.

Producing newsletters

These can be a very effective and inexpensive way of letting your customers know of your activities and that you care about them knowing. They can be produced quite easily on a computer and need not be highly professional in their presentation. The newsletter should be lighthearted and semi-informative and should be used to bring attention to any special offers from principals.

A typical newsletter is shown in Figure 16 and further reading may be obtained in '*How to Publish a Newsletter*' by Graham Jones in this series.

Mailshots from a principal

Many principals will have the ability to send their own mailshots to both your customers and any lists of prospective customers they may purchase. Try to make sure that he co-ordinates these mailshots with your efforts. It can be very frustrating to be diverted from a planned activity to deal with the inevitable enquiries these bring.

You may be asked for advice on the context and wording of the mailshot. The following points on mailshots from you should be borne in mind.

Mailshots from the agent

This is an excellent way of getting new information across to all your customers more quickly and far more cheaply than calling on them all. They can be achieved by using a suitable word processor

Terry James Agencies

Tel: 01905 840340

ON A PERSONAL NOTE FIRST!

N
E
W
S
L
E
T
T
E
R

I am happy to report that I am now 'on the mend' and the insulin injections seem to be working OK. Many thanks to the people who have telephoned with best wishes. I am now back at work and pestering everyone for orders. If I do go a bit funnier than usual just put it down to the Diabetes and rummage in my pocket (not my wallet) for a Glucose Tablet and give it to me wrapped in an order. The bigger the order the swifter the recovery!

TOR COATINGS LIFT LONDON

I am pleased to inform you that Tor (who purchased London Chemical Co), are increasing their stock levels of much of the LCC product range. The delay has been due to the need to convert the formulae to suit a mass production environment rather than the 'made to order, just in time' philosophy of LCC.

This will mean that all the mainline products will be off the shelf with overnight delivery if required, (at a small extra cost).

My Bottle of Moet & Chandon challenge to any customer who can tell the difference between ELASTASEAL 20 and another well known brand of a Moisture Trigger Polyurathane Roof Coating, will have to go on hold till I am back at work. I have carried out some six or so challenges and I have not had to cough up the 'Champers' yet.

As a matter of interest, a customer has found a new use for WP30 (a product for waterproofing Bricks, Concrete etc) He has used it, after a prolonged trial, on the concrete floor around a Fast Food Bar in Newport Bus Station. It seems they had a problem cleaning the area due to the greases and fats being 'ground in' by foot traffic. Two coats of WP30 did the trick and I am now told you can eat off the floor (!)

A TOR Product that may be of interest to some customers is an ANTI-CLIMB PAINT. This can be coated on parapets, downpipes etc and will deter vandals and coatings salesmen from gaining access to the buildings under your control.

BILCO COMES OUT ON TOP

Bilco (UK) have just gained a substantial order for Smoke Vents and Roof Access Hatches for use on the new British Library. Smoke Venting is being used in an increasing number of buildings in line with the long known dangers of smoke inhalation.

In fact, in the United States, where Bilco originated, smoke venting is the norm. The first thing a Fireman does on arrival at a fire in the States is to vent the fire

Unfortunately I was not involved in the sales on this project or I would be writing this from somewhere in the Bahamas.

The only interesting installation I have been involved in lately are a pair of very large Pit Access Doors for Severn Trent Water. These had to withstand a 16 Ton Axle loading and yet be opened easily by one man. This was easily achieved with one arm to spare.

Incidently, Bilco is spelt with a 'c' unlike Sergeant Ernie Bilko who spells his name with a 'k'. Also, when you get to know Bilco they are a lot funnier and have been established far longer.

HEAVY DUTY PIT DOORS FOR SEVERN TRENT

Money Saving Ideas Overleaf

Fig. 16. A typical agent's newsletter.

with a mail-merge facility on a computer, or by giving your mailshot letter and a list of customers to a bureau. The latter will, of course, be more costly.

It is important that, with existing customers, you address the greeting in the letter to the customer in the form you usually use to greet him. It is a bit absurd to address the letter 'Dear Sir' when you have greeted the customer as 'Fred' for the past ten years. By all means address prospective customers as 'Dear Sir': it is respectful to do so.

For further reading on this subject an excellent book has been written called '*How to Write Sales Letters that Sell*', by Drayton Bird, published by Kogan Page Ltd.

Above all, your mailshot should inform and invite some form of action from the customer such as 'telephone me on 01545 778990' or 'speak to Julie Wright'.

PROMOTING YOUR FULL RANGE

The advantage you have over employed salespeople is that you have more than one product or product range to sell. This advantage increases where you can sell more than one product to an individual customer. This initially calls for a lot of trust on your customer's part but, providing you have chosen your agencies carefully and that he is happy with the second product sold him, he will come to rely on you for even more products you may offer.

This is when an agent really comes into his own. Use every opportunity to show him new products, even consult him on any new agency you are thinking of taking on. Do not betray this trust by selling him something you are not fully satisfied with. It takes a long time to build up this trust but only one bad sale to ruin it.

HELPING YOUR PRINCIPAL GET PAID

Some customers run into cash-flow problems from time to time. It is a good tactic to get your principal to contact you whenever he is worried about a payment from your customer, before he sends a threatening legal letter. You can then approach the customer in a quiet and appropriate manner. Explaining to the customer that you will not get paid if he defaults will usually bring results, but not necessarily quick results.

Dealing with disputed invoices

It is in your best interests to see that your principal gets paid. Make sure that, if the money is in dispute, you help both parties to resolve the dispute. This may take some time and effort but it is partly your money they are in dispute over.

Handling complaints

This is a very important and sensitive area for a sales agent. He must do all he can to resolve the complaint from an individual standpoint and remember that, even if the complaint is unjustified, the customer thinks it is justified. The agent must take the matter up with the principal promptly and monitor the results. Promptly dealing with complaints is one way of preventing them snow-balling. Figure 17 shows correspondence from Charles Gann to a principal in which he is trying even-handedly to sort out a dispute between supplier and customer.

Not overcommitting principals

It is a wise rule never to commit a principal to an action without contacting him first.

Typical unauthorised promises can include:

- special samples
- fast deliveries
- product changes
- service visits
- special prices
- longer credit terms.

Should the agent be foolish enough to make unauthorised promises on behalf of the principal in such areas and the principal does not, or cannot, agree, the agent's credibility suffers with both parties. From the customer's viewpoint the agent made the promise which the agent cannot keep. From the principal's point of view the agent has made a promise which the principal cannot keep.

Howard Manufacturing
Wood End Works
Woodley
Reading
RG3 7YD   6th June 199X

For the attention of George Robson, Sales Manager.
Dear George
                    Re Granville Metering, Basingstoke.
                    Our Delivery Note: T5409: 1/5/9X
It appears that the goods that were delivered on the above delivery arrived extremely damaged
and are unusable by the customer.
The customer is asking for an immediate replacement on a free of charge basis.

I have told him that you will, most probably, replace the goods with an invoice and then
credit the original invoice when you have had a chance to inspect the goods and, if necessary,
claim off the carrier.

Could you telephone Fred Harrison of Granville on 01256 67890 and confirm your actions?

Could you also arrange the uplift of the alleged damaged goods?

Yours truly

Charles Gann

Fig. 17(a). Notifying a principal of a complaint.

Mr J Monckton, Managing Director.
Howard Manufacturing Ltd.
Wood End Works.
Woodley.
Reading. RG3 7YD   6th June 199X

Dear John
                    Re complaint: Granville Metering Ltd.
As you know, we both have had discussions with Fred Harrison of the above in an attempt
to satisfy his claim regarding the damaged delivery last month. Thus far we have not been
able to reach agreement with him regarding the payment for these goods.

This letter is an attempt to reach an agreement between both parties before he takes his
business elsewhere, which he has already threatened.

I can see merit from both sides. He should not have signed for the consignment as in 'Good
Condition' and Howard Manufacturing could have possibly packed the goods more securely.

As both parties are possibly to blame, could I suggest that you meet each other half way on
the disputed amount? I am sure that this will enable us to continue to trade with Granville
Metering and we can soon recoup your costs.

If you do take up this suggestion I will promise you I will try my best to get extra business
from them to enable you to get these costs back more quickly than otherwise.

I would be grateful if you could let me know your intentions.

Yours truly

Charles Gann

Fig. 17(b). Dealing with a customer complaint.

QUESTIONS AND ANSWERS

Q. *My major principal has issued me with visiting cards, describes me as his representative and generally avoids referring to me as an agent. He treats me as a paid representative. What should I do?*

A. Use every opportunity to tell and show your customer that you are an independent agent. Your principal might not like it but, as he is not employing you, he will have to accept it. Failure to stress your independence will lead to difficulty in introducing other products to your existing customers.

Q. *My new principal wants to do a mailshot to my existing customers. Do I give him a list?*

A. You will both benefit from this operation so it is quite in order. Remember, these are your customers and it is your relationship with them that is the important factor. He is, to them, a third party. Also make sure that there are many names that you would **like** to be your customers on the list.

Q. *My principal is refusing to continue dealing with a customer who is disputing an invoice. The customer is right. What do I do?*

A. Diplomatically take the customer's side without upsetting the principal. It will be a difficult task but a necessary one. Always be seen as acting as an intermediary.

CASE STUDIES

Charles maintains his independence

Charles Gann found that, once he was selling again, he thoroughly enjoyed himself. As it had been a long time since he had spoken to his previous customers he did not feel embarrassed about approaching them and selling the products of his new agency.

He found that most of them were genuinely interested in what he was doing and readily agreed to see him and the product. He felt a lot of satisfaction when the majority of them gave him a trial order on his first visit. His principal rang him after the first month and stated how pleased he was.

Charles found great difficulty in portraying himself as an independent salesman. Due to his lifelong role as an employed salesman he slipped into referring to his principal's company as 'we, us and ours'. The fact that the principal had furnished him with visiting cards with the company's logo on them and referring to Charles as their representative did not help. He decided he would print his own cards, describe himself as 'agent' and put the principal's company name in the top corner, leaving room for other company names at a future date.

Dennis's situation deteriorates

Dennis Wilson found that he was met with a certain amount of hostility from some prospects on the few calls he was able to make. It seemed that some of these people had already dealt with the company and had outstanding complaints that were, they said, being ignored.

Dennis took a note of the complaints and said he would take them up with the company. He then tried to sell them a new product from the company without success. He had not earned any commission on his first month's work.

He had a telephone call from the principal who wanted to meet him and discuss his lack of sales. They duly met and Dennis confronted him with the customer complaints. The principal told him he should be ignoring these complaints and that Dennis should be finding new prospects.

It was during this meeting that Dennis found out that they had started another agent on his territory.

Samantha uses her skills

Samantha Grey decided to use the computer to send out some mailshots to prospects telling them of her appointment as an agent for the two companies, outlining the service she could give them and telling them she would be in touch in the near future.

The setting up took some days but she felt it would be worth it in the long run. She obtained the names and addresses from the local telephone directory and addressed the letter to the managing director in each case.

About three days after they should have received the mailshot she telephoned each recipient and asked for an interview. Many of them told her that they had no use for what was on offer. Some said that they would like to see her and others said they were quite

A.B. MARKETING

(Proprietor: S.A.Grey)
36 Westwood Drive
Sutton Coldfield
W.Mids
B31 7YG

Mr H. Abblett, Head Buyer
Womens Fashion Group
Gresham House
123 High St
Warwick, LS12 5RF

Tel: 0121 403 133655

Date as postmark

Dear Mr Abblett

As you know I have been calling on you for some time now and I thank you for the business you have placed with me. Your sales of the Quagliotti Perfume range are up considerably which demonstrates the marketing skills of your company.

I have just been appointed as the sales agent for Gem Cosmetics in your area.

As you know, Gem Cosmetics have an extremely high profile in the market and are just about to embark on a 3 million pound promotion of their products. I am sure that you would like to share in the benefits this could bring.
The promotion will take place in:

● the major fashion magazines.
● television advertising.
● in-store demonstrations.

Gem Cosmetics will be sending you a separate marketing package at the end of June.

I would like to enter discussions with you earlier than this as Gem are offering generous discounts to pre-launch customers.

To this end the writer will telephone you during week commencing 30th June.

Yours sincerely

Samantha Grey

Fig. 18. A typical sales agent mailshot.

satisfied with their existing supplier. She made appointments with those who were interested and those who said they were satisfied with the existing suppliers.

She got the appointments with the latter by asking 'what would happen if your existing supplier let you down? Who would you go to?' Samantha was showing what an excellent saleswoman she was and how wise she was to have taken her career into her own hands.

Some months later, Samantha was able to send out a second mailshot to existing customers, informing them of a new agency she had acquired, and asking for an appointment to discuss possible benefits to her customers (see Figure 18).

Discussion points

1. How would you go about stressing your role as an independent business person and why is this so important?

2. Why is helping your principal to get his monies so vitally important to you?

3. Do you understand the importance of not committing the principal to a course of action without checking with him first?

10
Looking Ahead

This chapter explores:

- increasing the geographical area
- expanding your product base
- taking on sub-agents
- employing salespeople yourself
- taking on overseas agencies.

All these are ways of expanding your business, if you want to, after you have become established and profitable.

INCREASING THE GEOGRAPHICAL AREA

This form of expansion has major benefits and major drawbacks. The chance to increase an area usually comes via a principal having an adjacent area vacant and asking you to cover that area.

The benefits are:

- you know the product sells
- you know how to sell the product
- profits from existing business.

The drawbacks are:

- escalating travel expenses
- increasing travelling time
- fresh prospecting needed.

If you are offered an increase in area by a principal think carefully and ask questions before you accept:

- Why is the area vacant?
- Is there undue competition?
- What existing business is there?
- Is the arrangement permanent?
- Is the area easy to reach?

As you have already learned, the less travelling time the more time spent selling. The addition of an area can actually decrease your profitability.

EXPANDING YOUR PRODUCT BASE

This is probably the most used and profitable strategy used by sales agents to increase their business. The importance of taking on products that can be sold to your existing customer base must be stressed. It is also wise to take on complementary products or services. For example, your credibility would probably suffer if you attempted to sell packaging machinery and life insurance to the same customer.

He would probably view you as an opportunist rather than an expert adviser on packaging machinery or insurance. Selling packaging machines and the materials that are used on them can be seen as a logical step.

The exception to expanding in your chosen market sector is where you have made a conscious decision to leave that sector. Such decisions must be thought out carefully before any move is made.

TAKING ON SUB-AGENTS

With the level of commissions generally paid to sales agents, there is rarely enough margin to take on sub-agents and pay them a decent commission. Such arrangements rarely last long and can pose a threat to your relationship with your principal. Remember, you have no major control over a sub-agent's activities and his actions could jeopardise your principal's objectives.

If you do decide to go down this route to expansion, discuss this with the principals concerned and do make sure that the agreement you have with the sub-agent is written and in such terms as to protect your relationship with those principals.

EMPLOYING SALESPEOPLE YOURSELF

Some sales agents find that they have created more business than they have time to handle. Others may feel that, due to age or physical limitations, they want to take a less direct role in the business they have created.

This is when the question of employing salespeople crops up. This is a major step in the expansion of the business and the whole philosophy changes. An agent must realise that should he take this step he is losing his independence and that managing his employees will be an extra burden. The needs of his employees will dictate the direction of his business to a certain extent.

Most sales agents do not go down this route due to their overriding desire for independence. It mostly appeals to the younger agent whose desire, above all else, is to found a successful larger business.

TAKING ON OVERSEAS AGENCIES

An extremely high proportion of sales agents act as agents to overseas companies. Many overseas companies want to export to the UK and using sales agents is a logical first step for them. Many overseas companies may be looking for some form of stockholding so, in reality, are looking for distributors.

Nevertheless there are many good 'sales only' opportunities provided the product can be delivered from the principal in the time required. Many successful UK companies have started with a sales agency from an overseas company, progressed to a distributorship with financial help from the principal and then into a UK division of the principal with the UK directors holding a large stake.

Places to look for overseas agencies

- UK trade shows
- overseas trade shows
- commercial section of foreign embassies
- British Agents Register
- local Chamber of Commerce
- national newspapers.

Possibly the best route is to go to trade shows either in the UK or abroad. Here the potential principal has set out his wares and you can assess many of the criteria we have already established, easily and quickly. It must be borne in mind that the principal is obviously on his 'best behaviour' at such shows and that a slick presentation cannot address potential problems such as deliveries, creditworthiness etc.

Many innovative ideas do come from other countries but it must be remembered that innovation needs pioneering with its attendant financial risk. Do not be too impressed by a product or service that needs pioneering. This is not an area where a sales agent is at his best. Let others spend the money establishing the innovative product; you, as an agent, can possibly follow on after watching progress carefully. You will not make the fortune but there is rarely a fortune there. On the other hand your business will not fail due to the risks involved.

QUESTIONS AND ANSWERS

Q. *I have been offered an addition to my area that has far more potential than my existing area. Should I automatically accept it?*

A. You must evaluate the effects of the extra travelling, the extra time involved and the effect on your existing customers who are bringing you your existing income.

Q. *I have a son who has just left school and wants a job. Should I employ him?*

A. There are many excellent agencies where the whole family is involved. Good principals applaud this because it offers them continuity. The downside is that it is hard to sack a member of your own family.

Q. *I am a new agent and I am being offered an agency from overseas. Should I take it?*

A. It would be preferable to have become established as an agent and learned the necessary skills first. Nevertheless, providing that you can cope with dealing with your principal in another country, there is no reason why not.

CASE STUDIES

Charles reaps his rewards

Charles Gann had spent several years gradually increasing his agencies' turnover. He had taken on another three agencies and felt that the time had come when he wanted to expand his agency in order that he might start winding down his activities towards his retirement. He realised that he would need to employ either a younger salesperson or a sub-agent. He decided to employ a salesperson as he would have more control over his or her activities.

He also realised that he needed at least one other agency to support the financial implications of employing someone. He had seen an imported product that fitted in with his product range. He made enquiries at his local Chamber of Commerce, found the name and address of the foreign company and wrote to them. He wrote to them, enclosing his company profile in their own language using an interpreter suggested by the Chamber of Commerce.

He received a telephone call from them and was pleased to find that they spoke perfect English. They invited him to visit them and discuss the possibilities of an agency.

During the flight, Charles thought back to the long time ago when he was worried about striking out on his own. He realised that, with confidence in his own abilities, an ability to work hard and take disappointments in his stride, he had entered the most enjoyable phase of his life.

Dennis learns his lesson

Dennis Wilson had become completely disillusioned with the company he was an agent for. They were only interested in earning a profit for themselves and did not care about their customer credibility. Most of the salespeople who had been on the sales course with Dennis had already given up the agency. He was trapped because he still had to pay for the car.

Dennis realised that he had been too hasty when assessing the agency and had ignored the warning signs. He decided that he would give up trying to earn a living as an agent and seek paid employment.

He decided that the business of the payment for the car would be best handled by a solicitor. For once Dennis had started to think deeply about the consequences of any action he took. He is now a sadder and wiser man.

Samantha profits from her success

Samantha Grey did extremely well selling for both the agencies. One of the agencies was so pleased that they offered her an extension to her territory. The agent from the adjacent area was retiring and had a lot of customers who needed regular calling.

Samantha looked at the figures with the principal before accepting and noticed that the area on offer was in fact producing more commission than her own. There was a financial penalty in that there was extra travelling but the offer was still profitable.

She gladly accepted and is extremely busy and profitable. She thought afterwards that it was her very success as an agent that led to her being offered the extra success of proven profitable expansion.

Discussion points

1. Where do you see yourself in, say, ten years time and what do you want to achieve?

2. Would you have made the same decision as Dennis Wilson to seek paid employment or would you have tried again?

3. Do you realise that as a sales agent there is no upper limit to your earnings if you work hard at it?

Appendix 1

SUMMARY OF THE EC DIRECTIVE ON AGENCY AGREEMENTS

This summary outlines the parts of any agency agreement that are now enshrined in law. The directive does not cover every aspect of an agency agreement. It must be noted that all of the directive is assumed to be part of any qualifying agency agreement whether it is written into the agreement or not. It is not possible for either party to 'opt out' of any of the clauses.

A full copy of the directive and further reading may be obtained from the British Agents Register whose address is in the 'Useful Addresses' section of this book.

It is suggested that the interpretation of the directive should be addressed to legal practitioners. The British Agents Register also provide a free legal advice scheme for their members.

The EC directive deals with the:

- definitions of an agent
- duties of both parties to each other
- remuneration issues
- termination of agency
- entitlement to compensation
- rights to a written agreement
- restraint of trade clauses

Definitions of a commercial agent

The definition is 'a person, howsoever he may be described in the agency contract, who is self-employed and has the authority to negotiate the sale or purchase of goods, but not services, on behalf of the principal'. Agents selling services are thus outside the directive.

Duties of each party to each other

The agent shall:

- look after the interests of his principal
- act dutifully and in good faith
- make proper efforts to negotiate sales
- communicate necessary information
- comply with reasonable instructions.

The principal shall:

- act dutifully and in good faith
- provide documentation for the goods
- provide necessary information
- inform the agent of any refused orders
- notify any expectation of lower business volume.

The remuneration of agents

In the absence of any agreement the agent shall be entitled to:

- the usual commission on his area for his type of goods, or
- reasonable commission
- commission on sales during his agreement
- commission on sales due to his efforts
- commission on sales on an exclusive area.

Payment of commission is due:

- when the principal executes the transaction
- when the principal should have executed the transaction
- not later than the last day of the month following the quarter in which it is due
- commission shall be refunded if the right to it is lost.

The principal shall supply a statement on commission due not later than the last day of the month following the quarter it fell due and shall set out the calculations used to determine the commission.

The agent is entitled to demand that he is provided with all the information in order to check his commission, including extracts from the books and papers of his principal.

The termination of the agreement

The minimum period of notice of termination is, in effect:

- 1 month for the first year of the contract
- 2 months for the second year commenced
- 3 months for the third year commenced and subsequent years
- unless otherwise agreed the period of notice must coincide with the calendar month.

Your entitlement to compensation or indemnity

The directive allows for either compensation or indemnity to be written into the termination of the agreement. The choice between these is a fine legal point. Disregarding the differences between the two, there is obviously some form of financial redress for an agent being deprived of his agency.

It is generally conceded that compensation is potentially more beneficial to the agent than indemnity. Unless otherwise stated the agent is entitled to compensation rather than indemnity.

Ordinary commission is due after termination:

- within reasonable time if the sale is due to the agent's actions
- where the order reached the principal before termination.

No commission is due:

- to a new agent if payment is due to a previous agent
- if it is established the sale will not take place due to no fault of the principal.

If there is an indemnity clause
If the agreement allows for indemnity, the indemnity shall be paid:

- if the agent has brought new customers or significantly increased the business volume from the existing customers and the principal continues to derive benefits from this business

- on an equitable basis and taking into account the commission lost by the agent on such business.

The amount of the indemnity shall not exceed the figure equivalent to one year at the agent's annual remuneration over the preceding five years or, if less than five years has elapsed, the average over the years in question.

If there is a compensation clause
The following applies:

- the agent shall be entitled to compensation for the damage he suffers as a result of the termination.

The definition of **damage** is:

- when the agent is deprived of commission that he would have earned had the contract not been terminated

- where the agent has not been able to amortize his costs incurred in performance of the contract on the advice of his principal.

The grant of an indemnity does not prevent the agent from claiming damages.

The right to receive a written statement

Both the agent and the principal have the right to receive from each other a signed agreement setting out the terms of the agreement.

The restraint of trade clauses

A restraint of trade clause is where the agreement states that the agent shall not sell similar goods for a specified time after the agreement has been terminated.

A restraint of trade clause is only valid:

- if it is concluded in writing
- if it relates to a geographical area or group of customers
- if this area or group of customers is the same as that entrusted to the agent
- if it relates to the goods covered by his agency
- if it is reasonable to the agent, the principal and their common customers
- if it is no longer valid after two years.

CONCLUSION

This is only an outline summary given for information purposes. Should any query arise it is best dealt with by qualified persons. The directive has many words such as 'reasonable' which have yet to be tested in court.

The directive is particularly difficult to understand in the definitions of 'indemnity' and 'compensation'.

Appendix 2

A TYPICAL AGENCY AGREEMENT

The following is an example of a typical agency agreement. Every agency agreement is different due to the differing needs of the two parties. The example is offered as a guide only.

An Agreement made on the . . . . . . (date) between . . . . (the principal) whose address is . . . . and . . . . (the agent) whose address is . . . .

Appointment

1.1 The principal hereby appoints the agent as its sales agent for the sale of the products (schedule 1) in the territory (schedule 2), and the agent agrees to act in that capacity, subject to the terms of this agreement.

1.2 The principal shall not, during the continuance of this agreement, appoint any other person or firm as the principal's agent in the territory and shall treat the area as exclusive to the agent.

1.3 The principal shall be entitled to solicit customers and prospective customers on the territory and that where the principal does make such sale the agent shall be entitled to the commission, at the specified rates, on that sale.

1.4 The principal shall be entitled to declare certain accounts that pre-date this agreement as 'house accounts' and shall only be required to pay the agent a commission on these accounts at his discretion. The 'house accounts' are laid out in (schedule 3).

The Agent's Duties
The agent shall:

2.1 use his best endeavours to promote the sale of the products to the customers and prospective customers in the territory and shall act dutifully and in good faith.

2.2 keep the principal informed of his activities in respect of the product on the territory and shall every ... (length of period) provide the principal with a written report of these activities.

2.3 keep the principal informed of the conditions of the market for the products, of competing products and competitors activities in the territory.

2.4 refer any complaint or after-sales enquiry to the principal immediately.

2.5 only sell the products at the price specified by the principal (except by mutual agreement) and shall only use the principal's published price list to do so.

2.6 not be concerned, either directly or indirectly, with the manufacture, sale or promotion of any goods which compete with, or are similar to, the products.

2.7 not give any promises, warranties, guarantees or representations other than those contained in the principal's terms and conditions of sales.

2.8 give advance notice to the principal of potential orders to enable the principal to maintain adequate stocks of the product.

2.9 immediately pass any orders for the product to the principal.

2.10 comply with reasonable instructions from the principal.

2.11 not appoint any other agent or sub agent without the principal's approval.

Rights and Duties of the Principal

The principal shall:

3.1 act dutifully and in good faith towards the agent.

3.2 at his own expense, supply the agent with such samples, catalogues, price lists and promotional material as are needed for the promotion of the product.

3.3 provide technical and sales support if and when reasonably required.

3.4 provide all Health and Safety information when required.

3.5 provide product training for the agent.

3.6 inform the agent of any order that he is refusing.

3.7 notify the agent of any expected lower level of business from existing customers.

3.8 have the right to extend or alter the product range after having given the agent reasonable notice of his intention so to do.

3.9 give the agent reasonable notice of any changes to the price of the product to enable the agent to conduct the sale of the product in an orderly manner.

Financial Provisions

4.1 The principal shall pay a commission of . . . on all orders of the products delivered and invoiced on the territory (except the agreed house accounts).

4.2 The commission payment will be made by the last day of the month following the month of invoice.

4.3 The agent shall forward an invoice for his commission based on copy invoices supplied by the principal at the end of the month of invoice.

4.4 Should the customer default on the payment of invoices, after a period of 120 days from the date of invoice, the principal has the right to deduct the commission payment for that invoice from future commission payments, provided the invoice still remains unpaid. The commission payment will be re-instated when the customer pays.

Confidentiality

5.1 The agent shall use his best endeavours not to disclose any confidential information.

5.2 The agent shall not, for a period of six months after the termination of this contract, carry out any business similar to, or in competition with the products on the territory.

Duration and termination

6.1 This agreement shall come into force on the date hereto and shall continue in force until either party terminates in writing giving the following notice:

1 month's notice during the first year.

2 months' notice on the commencement of the second year.

3 months' notice on the commencement of the third and subsequent years.

Either party shall be entitled to terminate this agreement if:

6.2 the other commits any breach of this agreement that is incapable of being remedied within 30 days of notice of the breach being given.

6.3 an encumberer takes possession or a receiver is appointed over the assets of that other party.

6.4 the other party is made bankrupt.

6.5 the other party ceases, or threatens to cease, to carry on in business.

Commission on termination

7.1 On termination the agent shall be paid all commissions due to him under this agreement on the due date.

7.2 Should the principal terminate the agreement for any reason other than breach of this agreement by the agent, the agent shall be due compensation for the damage he suffers as a result of this termination.

Signed . . . . on behalf of . . . .
Date . . . .

Signed . . . . on behalf of . . . .
Date . . . .

Schedule 1   The products

Schedule 2   The territory

Schedule 3   House accounts

Glossary

Assets Items used by the company such as cars, computers etc.

Business plan Setting down on paper everything involved in starting the business, its strengths and weaknesses, running costs etc.

Cashflow The difference between the money coming in to the business and the money going out.

Compensation The amount due to an agent on loss of an agency through no fault of his own.

Drawings The amount you 'draw against expected profit' which is, in reality, your wage.

Commission Remuneration by way of a percentage paid on the invoice value of goods sold.

Database A computer list such as a customer list.

Distributor Someone who stocks and sells a branded product and earns a profit on that sale.

Exclusive area A geographical area, an industry or a customer type that qualifies for commission on all orders received by the principal whether obtained by the agent or not.

Hardware The solid parts of a computer system.

House accounts Accounts that the principal wants to retain without paying commission.

Indemnity A form of compensation for the loss of an agency.

Mail-merge Combining a customer list and a standard letter on a computer.

Mailshot A selling letter sent to a customer or prospective customer.

Principal Another word that the sales agent uses to describe the person he represents as an agent.

Restraint of trade Where one party tries to restrict the activities of the other after termination of an agreement.

Retainer A regular amount that is paid to an agent to secure his services apart from his commission.

Sales agent A self employed salesperson selling goods or services on behalf of another party.

Software The systems used on a computer.

Spreadsheet A computer generated table that is used for calculation and 'what if' calculation.

Sub-agent An agent that works on commission for another agent.

Tax assessment A hypothetical tax figure that the Inland Revenue will ask for in the absence of figures from you.

Taxable supplies In the context of VAT means any transaction that is taxable.

Tax year A year, usually starting from the date the business started, used as the basis for tax calculations.

Third party reference References made by customers known to the agent.

Unsolicited business An order that has been placed without the knowledge of the agent.

Word-processor A system for producing text on a computer system.

Further Reading

GENERAL

The Handbook for the Manufacturers Agent, C P Stephenson (British Agents Register 1990).
How to Start Your Own Business, Jim Green (How To Books 1995).
How to Start a Business From Home, G Jones (How To Books 1994).
How to Write Business Letters, Ann Dobson (How To Books 1995).

FINANCE

How to Keep Business Accounts, Peter Taylor (How To Books, 3rd edition 1994).
How to Manage Budgets & Cashflows, Peter Taylor (How To Books 1994).
How to Prepare a Business Plan, Matthew Record (How To Books 1995).
How to Raise Business Finance, P Ibbetson (How To Books 1987).

LEGAL AND AGREEMENTS

The EC Guide to Agency Agreements and Contracts (British Agents Register 1994).

SALES PROMOTION

How to Do Your Own PR, Ian Phillipson (How To Books 1995).
How to Write Sales Letters that Sell, Drayton Bird (Kogan Page 1994).

COMPUTERS

1995 Computer Buyers Guide, D Gibbons (Que 1995).
How to Manage Computers at Work, G Jones (How To Books 1993).

Useful Addresses

PROFESSIONAL ORGANISATIONS

British Agents Register, 24 Mount Parade, Harrogate, North Yorks
HG1 1BP. Tel: (01423) 560608.
Institute of Sales & Marketing Management, 31 Upper George St,
Luton, Beds. Tel: (01582) 411130.

SPECIALIST LEGAL ADVICE FOR AGENTS

Laytons Solicitors, 325 Clifton Drive South, St Annes, Lancs FY8
1HN. Tel: (01253) 782808.
Laytons Solicitors, Sunlight House, Quay St, Manchester M3
3LD. Tel: (0161) 834 2100.

TAXATION

Inland Revenue (Income Tax). See your local telephone directory.
HM Customs & Excise (VAT) See your local telephone directory.

ACCOUNTS SOFTWARE

Connect Software Ltd, 3 Flanchford Rd, London W12 9ND.
Microsoft Ltd, Wharfdale Rd, Winnersh Triangle, Wokingham,
Berks RG11 5TP. Tel: (01734) 271000.

BUSINESS FINANCE & HELP

Business Link. See your local telephone directory.

CHOOSING AN ACCOUNTANT

The Institute of Chartered Accounts in England and Wales, Moorgate Place, London EC2R.
The Institute of Chartered Accountants of Scotland, 27 Queen Street, Edinburgh EH2 1LA.

CREDIT CHECKING AGENCIES

Dun & Bradstreet Ltd, Holmers Farm Way, High Wycombe, Bucks HP12 4UL. Tel: (01494) 422000.

Index

How to Start Your Own Business
Jim Green

This dynamic guide fully explores the vital steps to creating a business, interlaced with the author's recent experience in overcoming every hurdle encountered along the way in setting up his own business without capital or discretionary resources. It will show you how to galvanise into initial action, how to source proven ideas, how to write a winning plan, how to approach potential funders, how to present a case for public sector assistance, how to market your business and how to develop the selling habit. No matter what your age or personal circumstances, you *can* strike out on your own, create an enterprise and change your life for the better. Jim Green is chairman and managing director of Focus Publishing International Ltd and for many years specialised in founding, buying and selling advertising agencies.

160pp illus. 1 85703 122 9.

How to Start a Business From Home
Graham Jones

Most people have dreamed of starting their own business from home at some time or other, but how do you begin? The third edition of this popular book contains a wealth of ideas, projects, tip, facts, checklists and quick-reference information for everyone —whether in between jobs, taking early retirement, or students and others with time to invest. Packed with information on everything from choosing a good business idea and starting up to advertising, book-keeping and dealing with professionals, this book is basic reading for every budding entrepreneur. 'Full of ideas and advice.' *The Daily Mirror*. 'This book is essential—full of practical advice.' *Home Run*. Graham Jones BSc(Hons) is an editor, journalist and lecturer specialising in practical business subjects. His other books include: *Fit to Manage* and *The Business of Freelancing*.

176pp illus. 1 85703 126 1. Third edition

How to Manage Budgets & Cash Flows
Peter Taylor

Today, it is not just accountants and book-keepers who manage budgets and cash flows. Increasingly it is a job for all business managers, whether in private firms or public sector organisations such as hospitals or schools. Written by an experienced chartered accountant, this new book provides a basic step-by-step introduction to practical budget and cash flow management. It covers planning, forecasting, budgeting, to monitoring performance, both as to current income, and as to capital expenditure on such things as new premises, plant and equipment. The book also covers VAT, costings and margins, and using computers, plus helpful action checklists and short case studies.

160pp illus. 1 85703 066 4.

How to Raise Business Finance
Peter Ibbetson

'Gives the right amount of information.' *Association of British Chambers of Commerce.* 'A lucid account of the steps by which a small businessman can substantially strengthen his case.' *The Financial Times.* Peter Ibbetson is an Associate of the Chartered Institute of Bankers, and an author and broadcaster on banking matters.

160pp illus. 0 74630 338 6.

How to Market Yourself
Ian Phillipson

In today's intensely competitive workplace it has become ever more vital to market yourself effectively, whether as a first-time job hunter, existing employee, or mature returner. This hard-hitting new manual provides a really positive step-by-step guide to assessing yourself, choosing the right personal image, identifying and presenting the right skills, building confidence, marketing yourself in person and on paper, organising your self-marketing campaign, using mentors at work, selling yourself to colleagues, clients and customers, and marketing yourself for a fast-changing future. The book is complete with checklists, assignments and case studies.

140pp illus. 1 85703 160 1.

How to Manage Computers at Work
Graham Jones

Here is a practical step-by-step guide which puts the business needs of the user first. It discusses why a computer may be needed, how to choose the right one and install it properly; how to process letters and documents, manage accounts, and handle customer and other records and mailing lists. It also explains how to use computers for business presentations, and desktop publishing. If you feel you should be using a computer at work, but are not sure how to start, then this is definitely the book for you . . . and you won't need an electronics degree to start! 'Bags of information in a lingo we can all understand. I strongly recommend the book.' *Progress/NEBS Management Association.* Graham Jones has long experience of handling personal computers for small business management. The Managing Director of a desktop publishing company, he is also author of *How to Start a Business from Home* and *How to Publish a Newsletter* in this Series.

160pp, 1 85703 078 8.

How to Keep Business Accounts
Peter Taylor

The third fully revised edition of an easy-to-understand handbook for all business owners and managers. 'Will help you sort out the best way to carry out double entry book-keeping, as well as providing a clear step-by-step guide to accounting procedures.' *Mind Your Own Business.* 'Progresses through the steps to be taken to maintain an effective double entry book-keeping system with the minimum of bother.' *The Accounting Technician.* 'Compulsory reading.' *Manager, National Westminster Bank (Midlands).* Peter Taylor is a Fellow of the Institute of Chartered Accountants, and of the Chartered Association of Certified Accountants. He has many years' practical experience of advising small businesses.

176pp illus. 1 85703 111 3. Third edition

How to Start Word Processing
Ian Phillipson

In the modern world an ability to wordprocess is a valuable, even essential, skill. It opens up new career opportunities, allows you to do your job so much better, and to complete all kinds of assignments far more quickly and effectively. Even if you know little or nothing about modern technology, this book will help you, because it deals with basic principles. If you want to design and print out simple letters and documents, produce mailshots, or explore desktop publishing, then this is the book for you, complete with case studies and checklists to help you on your way. Ian Phillipson is an experienced DTP and business consultant, with a range of business and professional clients in both the public and private sectors.

160pp illus. 1 85703 156 3.

How to Write Business Letters
Ann Dobson

Without proper help, lots of people find it quite hard to cope with even basic business correspondence. Intended for absolute beginners, this book uses fictional characters in a typical business setting to contrast the right and wrong ways to go about things. Taking nothing for granted, the book shows how to plan a letter, how to write and present it, how to deal with requests, how to write and answer complaints, standard letters, personal letters, job applications, letters overseas, and a variety of routine and tricky letters. Good, bad and middling examples are used, to help beginners see for themselves the right and wrong ways of doing things. Ann Dobson is principal of a secretarial training school with long experience of helping people improve their business skills.

160pp illus. 1 85703 104 0